DEPRESSION

The Essential Guide

Need
— 2 —
Know

Glenys
O'Connell

D1470608

First published in Great Britain in 2009 by
Need2Know
Remus House
Coltsfoot Drive
Peterborough
PE2 9JX
Telephone 01733 898103
Fax 01733 313524
www.need2knowbooks.co.uk

Need2Know is an imprint of Forward Press Ltd.
www.forwardpress.co.uk
All Rights Reserved
© Glenys O'Connell 2009
SB ISBN 978-1-86144-077-8
Cover photograph: Jupiter Images

Contents

Introduction

Depression is a word that is used a lot in everyday life. We say we're depressed if we don't get the job or the car loan, if we can't afford some item we've got our hearts set on, if we've had a fight with a friend or loved one; we even find some films, songs or colours depressing.

But what we usually mean when we say we're depressed is that we're feeling 'blue' or down. This is very different from true clinical or major depression. People experiencing clinical depression will tell you that it's as though all the colour has been drained from the world. They have trouble finding a reason to get out of bed in the morning; life doesn't seem worth the effort any longer and things that once interested or delighted them suddenly seem pointless. For the very depressed, even managing to get up and take care of personal hygiene is a major triumph, one which may seem beyond their ability as depression robs them of not only the energy but the desire to deal with their everyday activities. In a worst case scenario, a depressed person may find life not worth living and attempt suicide.

Most of us get over the blue feeling in a matter of hours or less and soon we're involved in some other activity and the dark mood is forgotten. But for the clinically depressed person, the feeling can drag on for weeks, months or years. It can be a steady drain on their inner resources and result in the loss of friends, job, career and lifestyle. For some, it can even end in suicide.

If you are diagnosed with depression, you should not feel alone. The World Health Organisation estimates that approximately 450 million people worldwide experience mental health problems, with depression being the predominant diagnosis. Recent studies indicate that approximately one in four women and one in 10 men in Britain suffer from depression at any one time. Statistics show anxiety and depression to be the most common combination of mental health disorders in the UK.

According to a report by the Royal College of General Practitioners, the estimated prevalence of depression in UK children and adolescents is between 2-6%. Disturbingly, the report suggests that most episodes of

'People experiencing clinical depression will tell you that it's as though all the colour has been drained from the world.'

depression in this age group last between seven and nine months, with almost half the patients experiencing a further bout of depression within two years and up to two thirds having a relapse within five years.

In the USA, it is estimated that each year 12% of women, 7% of men and 4% of adolescents experience depression – about 23% of the population.

Depression is in the World Health Organisation's list of top 10 disabling illnesses. According to a study by the World Health Organisation, 'Global Burden of Disease and Risk Factors' (2006), depression is the leading cause of disability for people aged 15 and older. However, it can be difficult to get an accurate international picture because in some countries mental health problems carry such a stigma that people are reluctant to admit to it, so the figure may be even higher.

You might be surprised to learn that depression is an equal opportunity ailment. Many well known people, from celebrities to political and business leaders, have experienced depression. Winston Churchill, whom some call the greatest ever British political leader, referred to his depression as 'a black dog' overshadowing his life. The famous artist Vincent Van Gogh is believed to have cut off his ear while in the midst of an episode of manic depression or possibly schizophrenia. The revered American president Abraham Lincoln suffered from 'melancholia', what we now call depression. Modern day writers Amy Tan and Anne Rice have both publically talked about their depression. Tan says depression exists in her family, while Rice attributes her depression to long term illness and grief at the death of her husband.

In the acting area, well known stars such as Hugh Laurie, Brooke Shields, Emma Thompson, Drew Carey and Harrison Ford have all battled with depression. In music, John Denver, Kurt Cobain, Sheryl Crow, Trent Reznor of the Nine-Inch Nails and Brian Wilson of the Beach Boys have all talked about depression and its effects on their lives. Even Buzz Aldrin, the celebrated American astronaut, admits to having experienced depression, as has footballer Terry Bradshaw. So, if you've been diagnosed with depression, you are in illustrious company.

'Many well known people, from celebrities to political and business leaders, have experienced depression. Winston Churchill, whom some call the greatest ever British political leader, referred to his depression as "a black dog" overshadowing his life.'

Depression comes in several different forms and degrees of severity. A key to coping is to understand what is involved, to recognise the warning signs, to know when to seek support and to get the kind of help you need. Armed with this knowledge, and an understanding of where and when to get help, you can begin to take back control of your depression – and your life.

Disclaimer

This book is only for general information about depression and is not intended to replace medical advice although it can be used alongside it. Anyone who is depressed, or suspects they have depression, should seek medical advice from a healthcare professional such as their GP in the first instance.

Chapter One

Types of Depression

What is depression?

It is only in recent years that people have talked openly about depression – it is a mental illness and as such carried a stigma in the past. There is no point in telling someone who is depressed to 'get over it' or to 'stop being so miserable, count your blessings' because they can't. It is an illness and needs to be diagnosed and treated with either drugs or counselling to help that person function properly again.

Depression can last for days, weeks or even years. People feel sad, lonely, cut off from other people and no longer interested in activities that once brought them joy. Each person experiences depression differently but the symptoms can range from constantly feeling tired, having no appetite or eating too much, being unable to sleep or unable to get up in the morning all the way through to thoughts or attempts of suicide.

Needless to say, depression has a detrimental effect on a person's life because it results in an inability to function at work, to study, to take part in family activities and a social life or to function sexually. It becomes a 'Catch 22' situation where the depressed person's sense of worthlessness is re-enforced as friends stop coming around, promotions go to someone else, exams are failed, dreams fall by the wayside and loved ones gradually lose patience.

While depression may be triggered by a traumatic event such as divorce, job loss, bereavement or a serious accident, this isn't always the case. Sometimes there is a family history of depression.

'I seemed to alternate between a sort of numbness: I could hardly be bothered to get out of bed, wash myself or even eat. I lost weight. Other times I seemed really happy but it was a happy like an over-stretched wire. The smallest setback would snap me into a temper tantrum. One day I got really angry with my son – I can't even remember what he did now – and slapped him hard enough to leave a bruise. I realised I was acting just like my own father had done and I knew I needed help.' Derek D.

In physical terms, depression is caused by an imbalance in the brain chemicals that affect mood and the sense of wellbeing. The main chemicals involved are serotonin and dopamine. Serotonin helps keep us calm, makes us less likely to be impulsive and helps us to be social. Dopamine covers our instinctive reactions, cravings, addictions and reward-activated behaviours. Normally these two drugs ebb and flow in our brains, balancing each other, and are regulated by messages flowing from neurons in the brain. In depressed people it seems that these neurons get 'stuck' and the chemical levels become unbalanced.

For some people, counselling sessions can help them to understand why they are depressed and the chemical imbalance rights itself over time. In other cases, drugs are needed to help the process along. For many people, a combination of drugs and therapy seems to work best.

Recognising depression and its symptoms:

You may be depressed if you have experienced two or more of the following symptoms in the past month.

- Feeling that you are incompetent and worthless.
- You take a long time to fall asleep, or sleep comes easily but you wake up in the night and can't get back to sleep. On the other hand, you could be sleeping much longer than normal and finding it hard to get up at the proper time.

- You've lost your appetite, even for foods you enjoy, or you know you're overeating. This may have led to a weight loss or gain that's adding to your unhappiness.

- You have feelings of anxiety, sometimes intense, but can't identify a reason.

- You feel tired all the time but your activities haven't increased to account for that.

- You aren't interested in your everyday activities, including those that you normally enjoy.

- You find you're disinterested in sex or even unable to function.

- You aren't taking care of your appearance or the cleanliness of your home.

- You feel generally unwell, have non-specific aches and pains, headaches or an upset stomach, yet you can't pinpoint a reason.

- You feel that your life is pointless and that you'll never achieve anything. You experience feelings of hopelessness and despair.

- You find yourself thinking about death and suicide a lot.

- You have mood swings or get angry and irritated over little things.

- Your sense of humour has deserted you and you feel like you'll never be happy.

If you have symptoms like these and they continue for longer than a couple of weeks, you should seek professional help. The best first stop is your GP. Make sure you get a check up to eliminate any possible underlying physical health problems that may be causing your symptoms, then the doctor can suggest treatment.

* The list above isn't intended as a tool for self-diagnosis – your medical practitioner is the best person to make a proper diagnosis of depression and suggest treatment.

Common forms of depression

The most frequently diagnosed form of depression is clinical or major depression, but there are a number of variations. The three most common of these are post-partum depression, seasonal affective disorder (SAD) and bipolar disorder (which is sometimes called 'manic depression').

Symptoms for all of these are similar but their causes may be different. For example, post-partum depression is triggered by childbirth.

Post-partum depression

'Sometimes called the "baby blues", up to 80% of new mothers report feeling sad, depressed, or having a low mood after giving birth.'

Sometimes called the 'baby blues', up to 80% of new mothers report feeling sad, depressed or having a low mood after giving birth. Many find this upsetting – after all, isn't childbirth supposed to be one of life's happiest events? They may feel guilty, alone, afraid of not being able to cope with the responsibility for this tiny new life or even afraid they won't be able to love their child. Fortunately, in most cases these feelings pass very quickly, usually within five days of the birth. Of course, it's something you should talk to your doctor about if it seems to continue.

But post-partum depression, sometimes called post-partum non-psychotic depression, is much more serious. While many new mums report feeling tearful and unable to cope at times, a woman with post-partum depression may also feel very inadequate, unable to concentrate, unable to enjoy activities, have a poor appetite or compulsively overeat and have thoughts of suicide. She may also worry unduly about her baby's health and wellbeing and be afraid she'll accidentally harm the child. These feelings interfere with her ability to look after the baby and bond.

In extreme cases, a new mum with post-partum depression may feel suicidal and consider killing her child as well as herself – not to hurt the baby but out of concern as to what will happen to the child if she dies. These irrational thoughts are rarely acted upon, but a woman experiencing these feelings should contact her doctor or health visitor to get help immediately.

More serious is post-partum psychosis, a rare condition occurring within three weeks of birth when a new mother may be agitated and can experience mood swings, sleeplessness, delusions and hallucinations. She may convince health workers that everything is well, but in reality she is severely depressed and may act on thoughts of hurting her child or herself. Again, it is very important if you or someone you know is experiencing these feelings that you seek medical help.

Adjustment disorder

Stressful experiences such as an unpleasant or frightening event can leave a person feeling drained, unhappy and depressed. These feelings can be easily tied into the circumstances. For example, being involved in a traffic accident can leave you shaken, uncertain about your own competency and can result in depression. Adjustment depression is milder than major depression and is your mind's way of coming to terms with what has happened. This type of depression usually passes relatively quickly.

Seasonal affective disorder (SAD)

We all know that feeling of being fed up with winter and wondering if the rain and cold will ever give way to sunshine and summer again. But for a surprisingly large number of people, the winter blues turn into something more serious – depression sparked by winter's lack of sunshine. It's believed that the lower number of daylight hours, possibly combined with lower levels of naturally occurring vitamin D from sunlight, causes an imbalance in brain chemicals, resulting in a mild level of depression that can last all winter.

It is recommended that getting outdoors, exercising, taking vitamin D supplements and even sitting under a sun lamp for short periods can help alleviate SAD.

'It's believed that the lower number of daylight hours, possibly combined with lower levels of naturally occurring vitamin D from sunlight, causes an imbalance in brain chemicals, resulting in a mild level of depression that can last all winter.'

Bipolar disorder (manic depression)

This form of depression has been romanticised in fiction because of the popular notion that some artists and writers create wonderful works during manic periods. Unfortunately, these works generally only seem wonderful to the artist while they're creating them – to the rest of the world, they may be unintelligible. When their mood swings into depression, the artist will see the work as vastly disappointing.

Bipolar means 'both poles' and this form of depression involves mood swings from euphoric to deeply depressed, sometimes within hours or other times lasting days. The sufferer may reach a point of physical collapse because of the heightened activity and sense of achievement during the 'manic' phase. The opposite or 'down' phase that follows can precipitate a depression so acute that suicide attempts may take place. A milder form of this illness, cyclothymic disorder, consists of similar but less extreme mood swings.

During the manic phase, a person may experience:

- Extreme happiness and excitement.
- Irritation with people who don't share this feeling.
- Heightened self-importance.
- A high level of creative ideas.
- An inability to relax or sleep.
- Fast speech and movement.
- Acting without considering consequences.
- Planning grandiose schemes without seeing them as unrealistic.
- Being reckless and uninhibited.

The patient may also experience psychotic symptoms such as hallucinations, delusions about their own abilities, disconnection from reality or unreasonable frustration at being unable to carry through creative ideas.

The extreme highs and lows of bipolar disorder can be distressing not just for the sufferer but for the people around them. Fortunately, this illness once diagnosed can be treated with medication and counselling.

Dysthymia

Dysthymia is another form of depression. It can last for years and often goes undiagnosed. The sufferer may experience low level depression for a very long time, often over a period of years. This longevity of the illness and its low level leads to people assuming the low energy, lack of optimism, etc, is actually a normal part of the person's personality. However, the low level depression facilitates a dysfunction that prevents the dysthymia sufferer from reaching the highest level of their abilities, skills and ambitions. Once diagnosed, dysthymia can be treated, usually by psychotherapy. However, if after three months there has been no noticeable improvement, a course of anti-depressant drugs may be added to the therapy.

Creative depression

To end this chapter on a positive note: some people claim that depression can actually be creative. Some artists, writers and other creative folk who are traditionally considered to be mercurial in their moods claim to actually experience a creative 'down' time before inspiration hits. Perhaps this is a time when the conscious brain needs a 'time out' so that creative ideas can cook on the back burner of the subconscious mind. Certainly the period before starting a new project may seem to be a very quiet and lethargic time for some artists – sometimes to the point where they may actually despair that they'll ever be inspired again. Some report that they wake up one morning to find themselves full of enthusiasm for a new project and quickly enter the creative zone to produce work that seems to arrive almost fully developed from their subconscious. So, perhaps depression has a good side to it for some people!

'Some [artists] report that they wake up one morning to find themselves full of enthusiasm for a new project and quickly enter the creative zone to produce work that seems to arrive almost fully developed from their subconscious.'

Summing Up

Depression is one of the most common mental health illnesses, affecting as many as one in five people at some time in their lives. Everyone feels blue or down at some time, but when these feelings are intense and go on for a long time without any apparent reason then perhaps it's time to consider whether or not you are clinically depressed. When someone is depressed they find it hard to go about even the ordinary routines of their life. They may retreat from social contacts, take time off from work or have difficulty fulfilling their regular duties. They may lose interest in hobbies and projects that once excited or absorbed them.

Many depressed people say they feel intense sadness and feelings of being totally alone and unloved. Others report feeling that they have no reason to get up in the mornings, nothing to look forward to and nothing that they enjoy. Some even feel they are worthless and do not deserve happiness, that there is no meaning to life and a sense of not really connecting with the people around them.

Depression can hit at any age. If your parents suffer from depression, you are twice as likely to suffer from it yourself. Even children as young as pre-teen have been diagnosed as depressed. If the first onset of depression occurs early in life, there is a much greater chance that other occurrences will follow.

But it's not as bleak as it sounds. There are a number of ways of treating depression, from counselling or psychotherapy to get to the root cause of the problem, to drugs that will help raise the person's mood and get them back to being able to cope with life again.

Professionals generally agree that a combination of drugs with the support of a counsellor to work through the problems is the best course of treatment. It ensures that a person experiencing depression can recover and develop the necessary coping tools to avoid or reduce future bouts.

'There are a number of ways of treating depression, from counselling or psychotherapy to get to the root cause of the problem, to drugs that will help raise the person's mood and get them back to being able to cope with life again.'

Chapter Two

What Causes Depression?

Triggers

This is a question that probably has as many answers as there are people experiencing depression. The fact is that, so far, there's no known one-size-fits-all explanation. For some people, it seems as though there is no identifiable trigger for changes in the brain chemical balance.

That said, some biochemical changes can be identified and some people are more vulnerable to depressed moods than others. For example, if a close relative has experienced depression, you may be more likely to be diagnosed with it yourself. This may be due to proximity or a possible genetic factor. However, with some thought, many people diagnosed with depression can often pinpoint some trauma or stressful life event that occurred before they became ill. And it doesn't have to have been a terrible trauma, either.

Many of life's events are stressful even when they are joyful – childbirth, for example. Getting married, getting a promotion at work and buying a new home are all happy occurrences that can carry a high stress factor. If you are currently involved in any of these, it's wise to pay extra attention to a healthy lifestyle with good nutrition and to get plenty of exercise and sleep to ward off the possible stressful side effects.

Here's a list of some of the events that may trigger a depression reaction.

- Bereavement.
- Unemployment.

'With some thought, many people diagnosed with depression can often pinpoint some trauma or stressful life event that occurred before they became ill.'

- Childbirth.
- Marriage.
- Marital problems, divorce or separation.
- Physical illness or chronic pain.
- Loss of a loved pet.
- Moving house.
- Promotion or new job.
- Loneliness or loss of friends.
- Being the victim of a crime.
- An accident, even if there is no serious injury.
- Alcohol or drug addiction.
- Certain prescription medicines – always check with your doctor.
- Financial difficulties.
- Abusive childhood in the past or abusive relationship in the present.
- Low self-esteem.
- Winter blues.
- Physical milestones such as menopause with its hormonal changes.

As you can see, some of these triggers are inter-related. Can you add your own triggers to this list for discussion with your doctor, therapist or a close friend?

Triggers and vulnerability

Everyone is vulnerable to depression at some point in their lives. It's just that because of personal background, experiences, genetics or something that science hasn't yet pinpointed, some people are more likely to become depressed than others.

'I was sure there was something wrong with me. I was tired all the time and wasn't interested in anything. I cried a lot. A friend said I might be depressed, but I couldn't imagine why I should be. I had a great job, a nice home and a good marriage. Finally, when I began to have thoughts of suicide, my husband insisted I see a doctor. That's when I found out that you don't have to be poor, lonely, unemployed or have experienced a trauma to get depressed – sometimes it just happens.' Glenna J.

People most vulnerable to depression are those who may have:

- Already experienced one episode of depression.
- Have had low level depression for some period of time (dysthymia).
- Have close relatives who have experienced depression or a family history of depression.
- Anyone whose partner or close relative is suffering from depression.
- Children growing up, or anyone who grew up, in a household where one or both parents have depression.

Anyone who has experienced depression in the past may experience more episodes.

There is a school of thought that suggests that a person's attitude to life can prevent them becoming depressed – or help to prevent further occurrences. This is the Theory of Learned Optimism – that if you can train yourself to think positive rather than negative thoughts, it is less likely you will become depressed.

Typical depressed thoughts:

- I'm worthless.
- I'm not likeable and have no friends.
- I'm a failure as a parent/friend/partner/employee.

- I'm not very attractive.

- I'm stupid.

- I never get anything right.

- I keep making stupid mistakes.

- Life isn't worth living.

Compare these to optimistic thoughts:

- I'm a good human being.

- I may not have a lot of friends but the ones I have really like and support me.

- I try very hard to be a good parent/friend/partner/employee and that's all I can do.

- I may not be a great beauty but I make the most of what I have. Besides, looks aren't everything.

- I may not be in Mensa but I'm not stupid either.

- When I look at the good things in my life, I realise I must have done some things right!

- Okay, everyone makes mistakes – time to learn and move on.

- Life has its good times – I just have to hang on till it gets better.

Can you see the difference in the downbeat thoughts of depression and the upbeat thoughts of optimism?

It's also possible with negative thinking for your thoughts to become self-fulfilling. For example, if you miss out on a promotion at work, negative thinking would be: 'I wasn't good enough for the promotion. I don't have what it takes to be successful.' This kind of thinking becomes a self-fulfilling prophecy as you give up trying to move forward with your ambitions because you think you don't have what it takes, so why bother? You don't do your best work and appear disinterested and lack lustre to your colleagues and bosses. More constructive thinking is: 'I didn't get the promotion but the competition was strong. I'll continue to improve my skills so I'll do better next time.'

How family history can determine your risk factors

People who have a family history of depression have a greater risk of becoming depressed themselves. Scientists say this may be due in part to an inherited gene called 5-HTT which affects the levels of serotonin in the brain. Apparently, if you have inherited this gene, you're more likely to become depressed after a triggering life event.

People experiencing depression do have lower levels of some neurotransmitters – the chemicals that carry brain messages between neurons – such as serotonin and dopamine. What isn't yet fully understood is the cause-and-effect cycle: does being depressed cause the chemical imbalance, or does the chemical imbalance cause the depression? If it sounds a bit like a Catch-22 situation, that's because it is!

Back to that 5-HTT gene that is known to affect the levels of serotonin. We inherit our genes from our parents, so children of parents with depression may have a genetic predisposition for depression. Also, because we tend to model ourselves and our attitudes on those of our parents, we may also unconsciously pick up on the negative thinking that we see them demonstrate. However, like so many possible genetic inheritances, there's no hard and fast rule. Not everyone who experiences depression has a family history of the illness, and not everyone who doesn't have the family history is immune to depression.

Life event factors

Back in the 1960s, Drs T H Holmes and R H Rahe carried out groundbreaking research into the stress levels of various life events, and gave each event a number of points which they called Life Change Units. They theorised that the greater the number of these units a person experienced in the previous year, the greater the possibility of some mental health issues such as depression. According to Rahe and Holmes, if you've accumulated more than 200 life change units in the past 12 months, you may be at risk of illness.

'People who have a family history of depression have a greater risk of becoming depressed themselves. Scientists say this may be due in part to an inherited gene called 5-HTT which affects the levels of serotonin in the brain.'

Note that a number of presumably happy events are included in this list, such as Christmas and holidays, which carry a possible financial burden and potential for family strife.

The stress scale works by assigning Life Change Units to events from a person's previous year. These units are added up and the final score is a rough estimate of the amount of stress experienced and how at risk of illness the person is.

Score of 300+: at risk of illness.

Score of 150-299: risk of illness is moderate (reduced by 30% from the above risk).

Score up to 150: only have a slight risk of illness.

Life event stress scale			
Life event	**Life change units**	**Life event**	**Life change units**
Death of a spouse.	100	Trouble with in-laws.	29
Divorce.	73	Outstanding personal achievement.	28
Marital separation.	65	Spouse starts or stops work.	26
Imprisonment.	63	Begin or end school.	26
Death of a close family member.	63	Change in living conditions.	25
Personal injury or illness.	53	Revision of personal habits.	24
Marriage.	50	Trouble with boss.	23
Dismissal from work.	47	Change in working hours or conditions.	20
Marital reconciliation.	45	Change in residence.	20
Retirement.	45	Change in schools.	20
Change in health of family member.	44	Change in recreation.	19
Pregnancy.	40	Change in church activities.	19
Sexual difficulties.	39	Change in social activities.	18
Gain a new family member.	39	Minor mortgage or loan.	17
Business readjustment.	39	Change in sleeping habits.	16
Change in financial state.	38	Change in number of family reunions.	15
Change in frequency of arguments.	35	Change in eating habits.	15
Major mortgage.	32	Holiday.	13
Foreclosure of mortgage or loan.	30	Christmas.	12
Change in responsibilities at work.	29	Minor violation of law.	11
Child leaving home.	29		

Summing Up

Just about anyone can become depressed, given the right triggers. Some people are made more vulnerable by family history, previous depressive history or serious trauma. There are many life events that can spark a depressive episode, including life changes that are mostly considered joyful. These include childbirth, marriage, moving house and the extra responsibility that a career promotion brings. Negative triggers can include unemployment, financial problems, bereavement, relationship problems, divorce, difficulties with children and conflicts in the workplace.

It is important to understand this, and to know that your attitude towards them can sometimes make a difference between becoming depressed or coping. Try to recognise where you may be vulnerable and do something about these situations before they become serious enough to leave you feeling depressed. Take control of your responses to certain things – feeling in control is a good way to stave off depression.

Chapter Three

You're Depressed – What Now?

You've finally worked up the courage – and the energy – to talk to your doctor about the way you feel. Now you have a diagnosis: you are depressed. You probably have a mixture of feelings: relief that you know there really is a problem and it's not a more serious physical ailment; anxiety about how people will relate to you if they think you have a mental illness; fear that you're never going to feel any better.

Along with these emotions, there's probably confusion about what treatment you should choose. Many people today are reluctant to take drugs, especially if it's going to be long term medication. On the other hand, can talking about how you feel to a counsellor make you feel better?

Now that you have a diagnosis, you will have to start making some informed decisions about the treatment that's right for you, in consultation with health professionals. Don't be afraid to seek help, whether it's a heart to heart talk with a close friend or a consultation with your doctor or a counsellor.

'My grandmother was "bad with her nerves" and my mother had "low moods". No one ever called it depression when I was growing up because it was associated with mental illness and that was a stigma back then. When I got older and found myself having the same kind of mood swings, I put off going to the doctor or seeking any kind of help for years because I was ashamed. I regret that now – all that time when I was unhappy and made those around me unhappy. Finally, I talked to a counsellor and she suggested I was depressed. My doctor prescribed drugs and, with the support of my counsellor, I finally started living again. It was a relief to have it out in the open, and I'd advise anyone first of all to get help if you need it, and secondly, don't be afraid to talk about it. Depression isn't anything to be ashamed of. It's an illness and you can get help.' Jean H.

Drugs or counselling?

As discussed earlier, depression is different in each person and so it follows that each person's treatment needs are different. Life would be so much easier if there was a one-size-fits-all solution, but there isn't.

Your doctor will give you good advice – if you have concerns about drug therapy, then they're the person to talk to. Your doctor can also advise you about counselling and what facilities are available in your area. Some medical practices have an in-house counselling service. You can also do your own research and seek out depression support groups.

The role of therapy

If you suspect there is some past trauma in your life or if you know there is a recent triggering event that has sparked your depression, then counselling may help. Often called 'the talking therapy', counselling encourages you to look at the personal issues behind your depression. A counsellor will encourage you to talk and will support you as you find your own solutions to the issues bothering you. Please remember that your counsellor isn't an agony aunt; they're not there to give you advice but to work with you so that you are empowered in the knowledge of your problems and able to find your own answers.

To do this, a counsellor 'reflects back' things that you have said by repeating them back to you in a slightly different way. This helps to give you a new slant on things.

Most counselling these days is cognitive behavioural which is based on two schools of psychological thought. One is cognitive psychology, the other is behavioural psychology. Bring them both together and you can see how useful this is in psychotherapy. Cognitive means 'knowing' or understanding the reasons why someone feels as they do in order to bring about change; behavioural involves changing, adjusting or learning new behaviours. So, cognitive behavioural therapy involves finding out and then understanding why you feel the way you do, then working out a way of changing your behaviour to help you feel better.

Most counsellors teach their clients relaxation techniques that they can practise at home to improve their general sense of wellbeing and sleep patterns.

Sometimes a counsellor may recommend hypnotherapy to help a client dig deeper into the subconscious. In properly trained hands, hypnosis is a valuable tool which can help a person remember past incidents and feelings, and perhaps reveal the root of problems. For example, it is often used for phobias. Don't worry about the stage acts claiming to be hypnosis where people run around clucking like chickens or carrying out other embarrassing behaviours. Your hypnotherapist will explain to you that hypnosis cannot make you do anything you don't want to do or that you consider embarrassing or unethical. Some counsellors are trained in hypnotherapy, others refer clients to a trusted colleague.

'Counselling encourages you to look at the personal issues behind your depression. A counsellor will encourage you to talk and will support you as you find your own solutions to the issues bothering you.'

An example of reflecting back between a counsellor and client:

Client: I started to get depressed when my mother came to live with us.

Counsellor: Do you think having your mother live with you made you depressed?

Client: Yes, yes, that's right.

Counsellor: Why do you think that is?

Client: Well, for one thing there's a lot more work.

Counsellor: And the extra work is a burden that's making you depressed?

Client: Not really, I don't mind the extra work really. She's my mum. It's just that…well, she's so ill.

Counsellor: And seeing your mum so ill is making you feel depressed?

Client: Yes…yes. It's hard, you know.

Counsellor: That's understandable. It's hard to see someone you care about going through a serious illness.

Client: Yes…I'm so afraid.

Counsellor: What is it that you are afraid of?

Client: I don't know. Does that sound silly?

Counsellor: Not at all. Why is it silly to be afraid?

Silence.

Client: I'm afraid she's going to die and leave me alone! Whatever will I do without Mum?

See how the counsellor encourages the client to dig down until they discover for themselves that it's not the extra work of looking after their mother that is causing the depression, but their own fears of losing her?

It's important that you take your time and find a counsellor you are comfortable with. Remember, you're going to be opening up your life and feelings and discussing personal things that you might never have talked about before. Some counsellors offer a free first time meeting – not a counselling session but time for the two of you to meet and see if you're a good fit. You might want to meet two or three before you find the person you feel most empathy with. Counselling can be quite expensive but it may be covered under some health schemes. Many companies also include counselling sessions in their employee health insurance plans.

Your doctor will be able to recommend one or more counsellors that they think will suit you, and you can usually get information from health clinics or you can look in the telephone directory. You may even find that a friend can recommend someone.

Choosing the right counsellor for you

Don't be afraid to ask questions. Make sure you consider the following when choosing a counsellor.

- Some counsellors have very busy practices – will they be able to give you an early enough appointment or is there a waiting list? Will you be able to get appointments at a time that's convenient to you?

- Is the counsellor accredited in a way recognised by your medical insurance provider?

- How much do they charge, and is it affordable?

- If cost is a problem, do they have a sliding scale of fees geared to income?

- Don't be afraid to ask about credentials.

- Do you feel comfortable with this counsellor? Do you feel they let you speak freely without interrupting you? Do you feel they reflect back correctly what you are saying?

- What style of therapy is practiced? Can they explain their style and how it is suited to your needs?

'Some counsellors offer a free first time meeting – not a counselling session but time for the two of you to meet and see if you're a good fit. You might want to meet two or three before you find the person you feel most empathy with.'

Asking for references is problematic – counselling ethics stress confidentiality and so your counsellor can't give you the names of other clients as references for you to speak to.

It is important that you feel safe with this person and that you are sure confidences will not be betrayed. I always tell my clients that 'whatever is said in this room stays in this room. You can cry, laugh, get angry or say things that embarrass you or make you feel guilty and no one except the two of us will ever hear of it.' However, there may be some occasions when you will want your counsellor to speak to your doctor or another health professional, and many counsellors will ask you to sign a waiver to allow that to happen should the need arise.

The role of medicine

When you consider how different depression can be from one person to another and the differences in brain chemical imbalances, you can see why a broad variety of drugs have been developed to help with depression and, at the same time, why some drugs work better for one patient than another.

In the same way that the causes of the chemical imbalances aren't properly understood, the explanation for how antidepressant drugs work is also not fully known. There's no doubt that once you settle on the right drug and the right dosage, antidepressant drugs do work for most people. Antidepressant drugs have been in use since the late 1950s.

There are several classes of antidepressant drugs:

- Tricyclic drugs (TCAs), sold as amitriptyline and imipramine.

- Monoamine oxidase inhibitors (MAOIs). There are three types of MAOIs: phenelzine, sold as Nardil, and isocarboxazid and tranylcypromine, sold as Parnate. A third is moclobemide, a reversible MAOI, which acts by reversing inhibition.

- Selective serotonin reuptake inhibitors (SSRIs) were developed in the 1980s and are the most common antidepressants prescribed today. They are sold under brand names such as Prozac, Paxil, Luvox, Zoloft and Celexa.

'When you consider how different depression may be from one person to another and the differences in brain chemical imbalances, you can see why a broad variety of drugs have been developed to help with depression and, at the same time, why some drugs work better for one patient than another.'

- The newest class is the reuptake inhibitors which block the reuptake of different neurotransmitters (brain chemicals). Serotonin and norepinephrine reuptake inhibitors are becoming popular. (SNRIs)

One of the concerns about any drug which works in the brain is the problem of side effects. The latest antidepressants, SNRIs, appear to have fewer side effects than the earlier ones. However, SSRIs are probably the most frequently prescribed because they are less likely to cause a serious risk in overdose.

You should also know that some antidepressant drugs must not be mixed with certain foods. For example, if you are taking MAOIs, you should avoid foods containing tyramine which includes cheese, fermented soy products such as Bovril or Marmite and red wine.

Your doctor will discuss these antidepressant drugs with you and outline any possible side effects. Again, don't be afraid to ask questions.

One thing to bear in mind is that most health professionals would recommend that a client take both antidepressant drugs and counselling. This is obvious when you think about it: for many people, although depression is caused by a brain chemical imbalance, it takes a past or current trauma or stressful event to trigger it. While drugs can make the patient feel better quite quickly, working with a counsellor can help resolve the issues surrounding the onset of the depression and perhaps prevent a future recurrence. Also, if a person has a relapse into another episode of depression, antidepressants can be prescribed but counselling may prevent a relapse by helping to sort out the issues that caused the depression in the first place.

In addition, counselling aims to help the client develop coping strategies – the behavioural part of cognitive behavioural therapy – which will empower them to recognise and avoid triggers in the future. So while someone may have another episode of depression, they will be better equipped to cope and recognise the signs before the depression becomes more serious.

If you are taking medication, here are some tips:

- Discuss possible side effects with your doctor and be sure you know what the drug is and what it is supposed to do.

- Take the medicine exactly as prescribed for maximum effectiveness.

- Some medicines may interact with each other, causing unexpected and even dangerous side effects. Be sure your doctor knows if you are taking any other medicines and double check with your chemist or pharmacist.

- Sometimes herbal medicines, vitamin supplements and dietary variations, for example being on a gluten-free diet, may have an affect on the effectiveness of your medicine. Again, check with your doctor.

- Read the instruction leaflet that comes with your pills. If you feel unwell or suspect you are experiencing an adverse reaction or side effect from the drug, call your doctor's office immediately.

- Never change the dosage of your medicine, or stop taking it altogether, without talking to your doctor first.

- Never share your medication or take anyone else's.

- Remember that alcohol and antidepressants don't mix and can even be a dangerous combination.

Helping yourself – taking control of your depression

In 1983, Andrew Billings and colleagues carried out a study of about 400 people who were beginning treatment for depression and compared them to 400 people who had not been diagnosed as depressed. Their findings support the idea that there is usually a trigger for depression:

a) The depressed group had experienced twice as many losses, such as bereavement, unemployment, loss of income or divorce, in the previous year compared to the non-depressed group.

b) The depressed group had relatively more sources of long term psychological pressure, such as a medical condition, family conflict or workplace stress.

c) The depressed group had fewer emotionally supportive friends or relatives.

* Billings, Andrew, G., Moos, Rudolf H., 'Life stressors and social resources affect posttreatment outcomes among depressed patients', *Journal of Abnormal Psychology,* May 1985, Vol 94(2), 140-153.

10 things you can do to help yourself

You can improve your own chances of easing depression and avoiding a recurrence in a number of ways.

- Take care of yourself. Look after your health, avoid getting overtired, eat nutritious food and get exercise and fresh air.

- Always have something to do that you enjoy; start a hobby, join a club or take a class. This gives you a reason to get up in the morning and encourages you to socialise and build a circle of friends.

- Build your own support network. Let friends and family know that you suffer from depression, and work out a buddy system so that you have an understanding friend to call or meet with for coffee or a chat when you're feeling a bit down.

- Learn to recognise the triggers. Does family conflict bother you? Try to solve problems before they become a full-blown conflict. Do you have a toxic work colleague? Arrange your work so that you have as little contact as possible with this person and make yourself believe that this person's mean behaviour should not be taken seriously.

- Make a list of the good things in your life and the things that you can feel grateful for. Read this list often – you may be surprised how good your life really is.

- Realise that you are not responsible for anyone else's behaviour.

- Try to keep a positive attitude – you can override those little voices that whisper negative things in your ear with positive statements.

- Avoid recreational drugs and alcohol.

- Be kind to yourself – understand that it's all right to feel sad when you've experienced a loss, and avoid blaming yourself.

- Know when you need help and don't be afraid to ask for it.

'Build your own support network. Let friends and family know that you suffer from depression, and work out a buddy system so that you have an understanding friend to call or meet with for coffee or a chat when you're feeling a bit down.'

Avoiding further episodes

Work-life balance

One cause of depression is stress induced by overworking, but spending too much time working and not enough playing can also bring about depression in other ways. For example, if your family is complaining that they never see you because you're always too busy, then issues that would be solved in day-to-day interaction can fester and erupt into full-blown conflict, triggering depression. If friends stop calling because you're always too busy with work to relax and kick back with them – or, even worse, to listen and support them when they need you – then pretty soon you'll find yourself isolated and without the social support group that will help stave off depression.

Some people immerse themselves in work out of sheer ambition, but others do so in order to avoid facing problems in their lives, problems that don't go away and that will eventually scream to be dealt with.

One way or another, all work and no play makes Jack – or Jill – pretty miserable. Modern life has become very busy and demanding, and people spend more, rather than less, time working and even skip holiday time in order to keep up. No matter how much you love your job, you still need time for yourself, your family and friends, otherwise you can become jaded, lose interest in your work and depressed.

Keep a diary of how you spend time for a week or so. Are you putting in many more hours at work than you spend with your loved ones? How much time do you have for yourself to enjoy a hobby, exercise or simply relax and think about your life? Does a long commute to your job mean wasted hours, an early start and returning home too exhausted even for conversation?

If you answer yes, then it's time to take control of your life again. Try and get a perspective on your work and remember that, no matter how ambitious you are, you need time to relax and unwind so that you can return to work refreshed and energised. If you do nothing except work, your life can become one-dimensional. Consider learning a new skill just for your self-development and think about how your family and friends feel when you're never around.

'Try and get a perspective on your work and remember that, no matter how ambitious you are, you need time to relax and unwind so that you can return to work refreshed and energised. If you do nothing except work, your life can become one-dimensional.'

10 tips for busting stress and rebalancing your life

- Take breaks when you're working – get up from your desk or wherever you work and walk around a little, even if you only get so far as the water cooler.

- Go out for lunch, even if it means a packed lunch in the park. Sitting in the sun will boost your vitamin D intake, a natural antidepressant.

- Organise your workload by priority and be firm in putting the least important jobs off for the next day rather than working late.

- Block out time on your calendar for a meeting with yourself, while you plan your work and allot time for what you need to do.

- If you can, consider delegating some of your workload or share some of the mundane jobs with a colleague so both of you get finished early.

- If possible, give yourself a day off every few weeks. Call it a 'mental health' day and return to work revitalised. If you can't take a day, at least try to leave work a couple of hours early.

- If commuting is adding long hours to your workday, ask yourself if it's possible to get a job closer to home – or a home closer to the job.

- Are there any tasks at home or at work that you do out of habit but maybe don't need to do? Ask yourself if there is a way you can drop these time-eaters or find a more efficient way to clear them up.

- Take a holiday. Schedule time to be with family or friends, people whose company you enjoy and find supportive.

- Learn to leave work at work. What's the point of making time for your loved ones when work issues bleed into it and distract you?

Nutrition and exercise

A brisk walk in the open air, a kick-about game of football or 30 minutes in the gym can help lift your spirits as well as improve your health and looks. Exercise releases endorphins, brain chemicals often called the feel-good chemicals for their effect on the way we feel.

Look at your diet as well. Eating properly is essential to feeling healthy in mind and body. The essential vitamins and minerals in certain foods can actually help to balance those brain chemicals. A balanced diet with fresh fruit and vegetables, easy on the junk food and little or no alcohol will help maintain good health and a positive attitude.

Brain friendly foods

- Use fishy foods to help beat depression – salmon, anchovies, sardines and mackerel all contain omega-3, essential for brain function.

- A moderate intake of carbohydrates boosts your serotonin levels and helps lift depression. We're not talking white flour, sugar, cakes and sweets here, which will simply make you heavier, but complex carbohydrates such as whole grain bread, pasta and cereals, along with fruit and vegetables. These help maintain a steady level of brain chemicals.

- Whole grains also contain the important B-complex vitamins, as do chicken, bananas, avocado and leafy green vegetables.

- Brain cells, which are called neurons, are like the cells in the rest of your body in that they need protein to build and repair themselves and to function properly, so add meat, grains, vegetables, legumes and tofu to your diet.

Brain unfriendly foods

- It's not actually a food, but many people think alcohol makes them feel good and lifts depression. The effect may be fleeting – alcohol negatively impacts your body's ability to absorb vitamins, minerals and other nutrients.

- You might feel that the boost from caffeine makes you feel better, but in the long term caffeine can over stimulate the nervous system, making you anxious and worsening depression.

- Sugar can be harmful in two ways: the quick energy boost it gives is quickly followed by a slump that is particularly bad for someone with depression; too much sugar can lead to weight gain which wrecks your self-image and increases depression.

■ There are a number of dietary supplements which may be helpful. Talk to your doctor to see what they recommend and to make sure there's no conflict between the supplements and any medication you are prescribed.

Summing Up

Once you have a diagnosis of depression, you have the choice of either using antidepressant drugs or psychotherapy (counselling), and your doctor will be able to help you make this decision. Be aware that antidepressant drugs don't work for everyone – they are effective in more than one third of cases and partially effective in another third. But they work little or not at all in the final third. This is why most health professionals now agree that for treatment of depression to be effective, it is necessary to treat the causes as well as the symptoms. Counselling is often recommended along with a drug treatment programme.

'Antidepressant drugs don't work for everyone – they are effective in more than one third of cases and partially effective in another third. But they work little or not at all in the final third.'

For some people, particularly those with an identifiable trigger for their depression, counselling on its own may help. Weigh the pros and cons carefully and make an informed decision about how you want to proceed.

You can improve your own chances of easing depression and avoiding a recurrence in a number of ways. These involve taking good care of your health and nutrition, getting a reasonable amount of exercise and fresh air, keeping active with occupations that interest you or by taking a class to learn something new. You can also benefit from building a support network with friends who know you suffer from depression and who will support you in a 'buddy system' when you're feeling down.

You should also learn to recognise the triggers that bring on depressed feelings and then try to act to either avoid or solve the problems. Try to keep a positive attitude and understand that you can't be responsible for anyone else's behaviour. Last but not least, understand that alcohol should be avoided not only because it is a depressant but also because antidepressant medications and alcohol can be a dangerous mixture.

Chapter Four

Caring for Someone Who's Depressed

Like any other illness, depression doesn't just affect the person experiencing it. Depression reaches out its tentacles to family members, friends, co-workers and anyone within the orbit of the depressed person. Does that seem dramatic?

Imagine the husband or wife starved of interaction, affection and support. Imagine the child longing to play with a parent who's too depressed to respond, or once more telling a teacher that 'Mum's not feeling well and can't help out' at the school fair or other event.

Consider the friends who miss the shared interests and mutual support, and the co-workers who have to pick up the slack when work isn't done because someone is too depressed to show up.

'My mother cried a lot when I was little and she was always tired. Other kids' mums played with them and laughed a lot – my mum never played with me. I thought it was because she didn't like me, that she was somehow disappointed in me. I tried so hard to please her but nothing ever worked. I thought it was my fault she was unhappy. I thought if my mum couldn't love me, then nobody else would be able to either. It affected all my relationships. It was years before I understood that she was depressed and it wasn't anything I'd done.' Lesley H.

How you can help

Depression puts a strain on all our relationships. Sadly, it's when we are depressed that we most need the understanding of caring people around us, yet our depressed moods can drive them away.

- If someone you care about is depressed, you can support them just by being patient and loving. Understand that you are not responsible for their unhappiness and that withdrawing from them will actually cause further hurt rather than healing for both of you.

- Because a depressed person often feels overwhelmed by everyday responsibilities, try if you can to take over some of their daily duties until they are able to carry on.

- Don't criticise or complain, even when the passivity and tearfulness of their depression gets you down too.

- Work with your loved one to find constructive ways of helping them come out of the depression, perhaps by pinpointing stressful situations in their personal life or employment and looking for solutions. These situations may act as triggers for depression. For example, if you know this person hates confrontation and every time there's a family get-together there's a row, discuss this situation and perhaps avoid going to these events until they feel better.

- Encourage them to visit the doctor and/or counsellor. If the situation is really getting you down, ask if you can see the counsellor together for a session and explain how you feel. The counsellor may be able to suggest ways that the two of you can help each other.

- If your depressed loved one is taking medication, make sure they take the right dose at the right time. Offer to pick up renewed prescriptions, etc, so they don't run out of pills.

- Keep a watchful eye on them and look for any changes in the depressed mood. If you become alarmed that the mood is deepening or that the person is becoming suicidal, don't hesitate to contact the doctor or counsellor for advice. It is better to sound the alarm early and risk being wrong than to wait and risk the situation becoming critical.

- You probably won't be able to avoid getting irritated or frustrated at times, but try to discuss the situation calmly. Work together to find ways of making day-to-day life easier.

Remember that you need support too. Try to make time for coffee, an evening out or an afternoon shopping with a friend. Build your own support group of discreet people who will let you vent your feelings and know you still love your depressed partner.

Don't feel guilty. You may find yourself getting angry or wishing your depressed loved one would just go away.

Accept that you are also under stress because of the depression and make sure you get enough 'me' time when you can relax and enjoy some time away. This will help you recharge your batteries so that you can continue being a supportive partner or friend.

At times it may seem that your depressed partner is lazy, pathetic, selfish or weak and that their behaviour is screwing up your life. Bear in mind again that they did not choose to be depressed. The depression will pass in time and you'll have your life back with the person you love. In the meantime, it's important that you get on with your own life as far as possible to reduce the resentment that may build up inside you when it seems that their depression is dominating your lives.

'Build your own support group of discreet people who will let you vent your feelings and know you still love your depressed partner.'

Five things you should never say – and why

1) Get over it!

2) You're making everyone else miserable, buck up!

3) I'm so sick of seeing you like this.

4) I'm tired of being around you when you don't make any effort.

5) What have you got to be depressed about? Look at all the people worse off than you!

So why shouldn't you say these things? Depression is a mental illness and it's not possible to just 'get over it'. Depressed people need to feel loved, and fear of being abandoned will only increase their sense of worthlessness. Sadly, no matter how much worse off other people might be, someone in the midst of depression can't measure their lives like that. In fact, if said to someone who's depressed, some of these phrases only add guilt to their depression.

Be aware that people who live with someone who is depressed are likely to experience depression themselves, and children of a depressed parent are up to twice as likely to become depressed themselves. Make sure you talk to a doctor or counsellor yourself if you feel the need, or seek help for a child who may be showing signs of depression.

Talking about depression and removing the stigma

- Talk about depression and get your loved one to talk about it too. There's no shame in being depressed and the stigma of mental illness should be left in the past where it belongs.

- If your husband, wife or partner is depressed and you have children, do try to explain to them what's happening. Keep it suitable for their age group: often a simple 'Mummy/Daddy is not feeling well and that's why she/he is being so quiet' will be enough. Children don't have a lot of life experience and tend to jump to the conclusion that they are to blame if their mum or dad is unhappy. They think they've done something wrong, and if someone is too depressed to respond to them warmly, they may carry that sense of guilt with them into adulthood unless the situation is explained. They need to understand that what's happening is no one's fault and that life will eventually return to normal.

- If people ask, tell them that your spouse or partner is depressed. Explain that it's a mood disorder and that he or she is doing everything possible to get over it, but in the meantime you'd appreciate their support as friends and co-workers.

- Don't stop inviting people round or accepting invitations to visit friends. Going out and about may lift the mood for both of you. If you have children, it may be even more important to keep to a normal social and everyday routine.

'If I had a broken leg, everyone would see the big plaster cast and they'd feel sorry for me, come round and try to cheer me up. But no one can see my depression, I just look like a big soft misery guts who's a killjoy to boot because I don't want to have fun or join in anything. People find it hard to understand why I don't just snap out of it. I can't blame people for not wanting to visit and spend time with me when I'm so depressed, but I do wish they'd make the effort to come round sometimes.' Mary J.

There are support groups available in some areas – ask your local social services department, doctor, counsellor or church group if they know of one for people coping with depression. These groups offer advice and support for depressed people and often have support groups for friends and family too. You might find it helpful to talk to other people who are supporting depressed friends or relatives and your depressed partner will feel better knowing they are not unique in this condition.

Summing Up

It's a conundrum really: when someone is depressed, they seriously need the support of friends and family, yet the effect of depression is to drive people away. If you care about someone who is depressed, try to remember that they can't just pull themselves together or get over it. Depression is a mental illness and in most cases needs treatment in the form of medication, counselling or both.

Non-judgemental support, holding back your own frustration and criticism and encouraging your depressed partner or friend to seek help and take steps to ease their depression are important. Picking up the extra workload at home or at work is also a big help, as is trying to maintain a social life for the two of you. Work with them to see if you can identify situations that trigger depressed feelings and try to work out solutions. Encourage them to eat a balanced diet, take medications properly and to get out and socialise. Find out the name of the doctor or counsellor they are seeing and keep the phone number handy in case you need to call for advice.

If you have children, it is very important for their welfare to explain the situation to them in language suitable for their age group. Even very young children can understand if someone isn't feeling well, and you can work with them to help them see that they have done nothing wrong to cause their mum's or dad's sadness.

Last but by no means least, it is important to take care of your own health. Studies have shown that people close to someone with depression often experience depressed feelings themselves. Make sure that you, like your loved one, get enough rest, relaxation and good nutrition. Take time out so that you can visit friends or enjoy a favourite activity, and don't hesitate to seek help for yourself from a doctor or counsellor if you feel that things are getting you down.

Understanding depression and working together could bring the two of you closer than ever, enabling you to enjoy life even more once the depression is over.

Chapter Five

Depression and Suicide

In days gone by, suicide was considered shameful and a sin. Suicides could not be buried in hallowed ground and were relegated to unconsecrated ground outside the churchyard walls. A conspiracy of silence grew up, where doctors would sometimes pronounce a different cause of death to spare a family more suffering, or shamed families would hide the fact of suicide.

Society is more compassionate today, recognising that suicide has its roots in pain, suffering, physical illness, occasionally anger, but more often in mental illness, and that neither a suicide nor their family should be blamed.

Depression and suicide are often spoken together in the same sentence – thoughts of suicide are one of the items listed on the checklist for depression. This isn't without justification, because in patients diagnosed with major depression there is as much as a 6% risk of suicide over their lifetime. For a person suffering from bipolar disorder, that risk is much higher. In all circumstances, risk of suicide may be increased by alcohol or drug abuse and is if there has already been a suicide attempt.

According to the Samaritans organisation, about 10% of the population aged 16-65 in Britain reports symptoms of depression in any given week and a tenth of these admit to having thoughts of suicide.

It is, therefore, depression's darkest side.

'Suicide has its roots in pain, suffering, physical illness, occasionally anger but more often in mental illness.'

Suicide – depression's darkest side

Suicide is a double edged sword – not only is it tragic for the person who commits, or tries to commit, suicide, but it leaves a legacy of grief and guilt among the people left behind. They are destined to always ask themselves if there was something they could have done to save this person or if there were warning signs they could have seen and didn't. Sadly, these warning signs may only be evident after the fact, although this does little to ease the burden of pain on those who cared about the victim and were unable to help.

> 'I was usually the one who made sure my husband took the correct dose of his medication, but I remember being so tired and I had the flu. I went to bed early that night and because I was coughing so much I slept in the spare bedroom so I would not disturb his sleep. The next morning he was dead from an overdose. There was no note – I don't know if it was a conscious decision to take his own life or if he simply was so disconnected at that point that he wasn't aware of what he was doing.
>
> 'For so long it seemed that we were both running on my "life energy". I was the one who got up in the morning, made breakfast, took care of things. I repressed my enthusiasm at times because it simply didn't go with his depression. It was inevitable that I would reach a point where I could no longer continue to provide enough life energy for us both and I got the flu because I was worn out. Would he have overdosed if I had been well enough to see to his medication and be there? I think that's something I'll never know, but it seems as though it was inevitable that it would happen.' Hayley S.

'There are some indicators of a possible suicidal intent, including a sudden change of mood, giving away treasured possessions, even visiting old friends or relatives the person has lost touch with. There's a sense of making things right.'

Who's most at risk?

There are some indicators of a possible suicidal intent, including a sudden change of mood, giving away treasured possessions, even visiting old friends or relatives the person has lost touch with. There's a sense of making things right. Frequently, the suicidal person may even seem happier and more relaxed to friends and family because they have made a decision to end their life.

According to studies, people who display aggressive or impulsive behaviour, are addicted to alcohol or drugs, have experienced parental divorce or separation or who have a close friend or family member who has committed suicide may also be more likely to experience thoughts of suicide.

There's a saying that 'suicides come in threes'. Whether this is true or not, it appears that having a close friend or relative who commits suicide, or attempts to do so, can be a trigger for suicidal thoughts in other people, particularly in someone who is already depressed.

In addition, the risk of suicide is heightened in people who experienced their first episode of major depression in their teens, people who self-mutilate, people with schizophrenia and new mothers suffering from severe post-partum depression. The latter are at greatest risk in the first year following the birth of their child.

As you can see, depression is a component in all these additional factors, so suicidal thoughts should not be taken lightly or dismissed without some follow-up with a health professional.

Suicide risk factors

- Serious or chronic physical illness.
- Major depressive episodes.
- A history of self-harm.
- A history of alcohol or drug abuse.
- Schizophrenia.
- Having a friend or relative who committed suicide or has tried to.

Warning signs

The warning signs of suicide differ from individual to individual, and sometimes even close relatives and friends miss the clues until it is too late. Perhaps they are subconsciously ignored because the idea of losing someone they care about to suicide is too appalling to contemplate. Here are some of the most common symptoms that may be present in a depressed person considering taking their own life:

- Talking a lot about death, expressing the view that they don't expect to be around for upcoming events.

- Suggesting that their family or friends wouldn't miss them or would even be better off without them.

- Acting out of character or saying and doing things that they wouldn't ordinarily do, such as taking unnecessary risks, drinking heavily and driving too fast.

- Having no interest in planning for the future or setting up activities.

- Visiting relatives and friends that they've not seen for some time, perhaps trying to mend old arguments and set things right.

- Giving away possessions that they treasure.

'I felt as if everything hurt, not so much physically maybe as in my mind. The slightest thing, something someone said, whatever, left me feeling hurt and numb. And I was so alone – I knew no one understood what I was feeling. I got so that I'd stay in bed and daydream about not waking up in the morning. Finally, I decided that this just wasn't worth living with anymore.

'Funnily enough, once I'd made the decision it felt like a load had been taken off my shoulders. My friends say that night I seemed happy and relaxed for the first time in ages. We had a great night out. Then I went and got in my car, drove right at a tree – just my luck I hit a wire fence and stalled with nothing more than a bump on my head. Looking back, I say thank God someone noticed me. A guy out walking his dog late saw the crash and called an ambulance. But at the time, I just wanted to die.' L.J.

If you're having thoughts of suicide yourself, now is the time to seek help. Maybe you think you're all alone, no one cares if you're there, maybe you even feel the world, or the people you care about, will be better off without you. Take a step back from this. Remember that there is help for you and, if you hold on long enough, these feelings will pass. Think of your family, your friends. Do you really want to leave them with the legacy of guilt and grief that they will inherit if you exit their lives by suicide? Talk to your counsellor, to a close friend or relative, your teacher, school guidance counsellor, company nurse, your family doctor, the personnel officer at work or call the Samaritans or one of the other helplines and ask for help.

If you feel in immediate danger of ending your own life, visit the hospital's emergency department (or get someone to take you there) and tell the doctor on duty that you're suicidal. Do whatever it takes to get you the help you need – quickly!

People with bipolar disease are at greater risk of suicide. Studies suggest they may be 15 times more likely to take their own life than the general population. The risk increases if there has been a previous suicide attempt or if the person is drinking alcohol heavily or using 'recreational' drugs.

When to sound the suicide alarm

At this point you're probably thinking: this is all very well, but what can I do? If you think someone you know is thinking of suicide, then there's a lot you can do to try to stop them.

- Firstly, if they are talking to you about suicide, that's a cry for help and you may be the only person they're telling. Don't think you've got to keep this a secret, even if you make that promise to your friend. Talk to other friends and family members and express your concern.

- Try and get your friend to call one of the many suicide helplines or to visit their own doctor for help. Get other people to back you in this gentle persuasion. Don't wait and see if it will pass – if necessary, take the person to their doctor yourself.

- Don't believe the myth that suicides don't talk about their plans – most suicides have expressed their thoughts of dying before they try to end their lives. Is this because they want someone to stop them? Probably.

'Don't believe the myth that suicides don't talk about their plans – most suicides have expressed their thoughts of dying before they try to end their lives.'

What to do?

- Keep your conversation non-judgemental – a suicidal person has enough guilt, anxiety and feelings of worthlessness without being judged.

- Persuade them to seek immediate help – either phone the suicide helpline (in the telephone directory) and hand them the phone or, if you think it's urgent, get them to go to the doctor or hospital with you.

- Stay with them.

- Show them you are taking their feelings seriously and that you care about them.

- Tell them these feelings may be very real now but that they will pass and that problems can be solved.

- Even if their words shock you, keep your feelings to yourself.

- Make sure there are no guns, knives, medications or other things available that could be used in a suicide attempt.

- Unless you're a trained mental health professional, understand that coping with suicide needs special skills and do your best to get this help. Understand also that, in the final analysis, if someone you've tried to help goes ahead and attempts suicide, it is not your fault. Don't play the blame game with yourself.

Nine myths of suicide debunked

- People who talk about suicide don't do it.
  Any talk of suicide should be treated seriously. Most people who attempt to end their lives have talked or hinted about it first.

- Someone who wants to commit suicide wants to die.
  No, they just want to end the pain, emotional or physical, that they are experiencing. Death may seem to be the only solution to them at that time.

- Someone who's suicidal is always going to be at risk.

People usually consider suicide because it seems to be the only way out of a painful situation. If the situation can be changed, then the need to end their life may go away.

- Talking about suicide plants the idea in people's minds.
  Talking to someone shows you are concerned. Allowing them to talk about their feelings is more likely to help them find another solution or seek help than it is to validate their suicidal feelings.

- Once someone has tried to commit suicide and failed, they won't try it again.
  If nothing has changed and they've not solved the problems or received medical treatment and counselling, then they may well try again.

- If someone who's been threatening suicide suddenly seems happier, it means the crisis is over.
  It may just mean that they've made a decision to kill themselves and now feel better as they believe they can see an end to their pain.

- It's possible to identify the kind of person who will attempt to end their own life.
  While there are a number of factors and warning signs, there is no particular identifiable suicidal character type. Suicide often flows from depression and just about anyone can experience clinical depression.

- Most suicides follow through without ever asking for help.
  Most people considering suicide will have confided their negative feelings in a friend, relative or co-worker. Some may even have visited their doctor.

- There's no previous history or warning when someone is going to attempt to take their own life.
  Even though some suicides appear to be a spontaneous reaction to loss or trauma, there is frequently a history of mood disorders or life stress difficulties.

The controversy of antidepressant drugs and suicide

There is an irony in that while antidepressants are the main treatment of choice by doctors and they work for many depressed people, these drugs have also been used by a significant number of people to attempt suicide by overdose. It appears that older people, people with previous attempts at suicide and people who self-mutilate are most at risk. Although these drugs are effective in helping depression, researchers are still debating whether they actually help prevent suicide.

The SSRIs appear to be less likely to be fatal in overdose. However, these are not generally prescribed to young people under the age of 18 because they seem less effective, and because of fears raised by an apparent relationship between the use of SSRIs and suicidal thoughts and attempts in children.

An apparent increase in suicide when people started taking SSRIs has largely been dismissed on the basis that people starting medication are newly-diagnosed and in the deepest stages of depression and so more vulnerable to suicidal tendencies. Other suggestions have indicated that a possible increase in suicidal behaviour among people taking antidepressants may be due to the person actually feeling better. With the depression lifted by drugs, the patient is capable of making decisions – they may see that their life still has the same problems and decide to commit suicide. This is one of the reasons that counselling is recommended along with drug treatments as the most effective treatment for depression.

There are many ongoing studies regarding these issues but it is obvious that antidepressants, as with all drugs, should be used according to a doctor's directions.

It should be noted that there are claims that a number of other drugs besides antidepressants can cause chemical imbalances in the brain. These include a wide range of treatments for high blood pressure, obesity, acne, insomnia, heartburn and other conditions, prompting the UK government to require that every new drug going on sale must carry a suicide rating.

Advice for young people

Young people often talk to their friends about suicide – and those young friends may find themselves with a heavy responsibility. If you are concerned about a friend, here are some things to look out for.

Have they:

- Talked about death a lot?
- Talked about feeling hopeless or guilty, that life isn't worth living?
- Stopped socialising and mixing with family and friends?
- Lost interest in their usual activities?
- Started to get involved in excessive alcohol use?
- Started using illegal drugs?
- Shown problems concentrating?
- Experienced changes in eating or sleeping habits?
- Acted erratically or recklessly, like driving too fast?

What do you know about what's happening in their life? Get them to open up and talk about the things that are worrying them. Maybe they're going through a difficult time such as the break up of a long term relationship, parental divorce or bereavement. Have they lost a friend or relative to suicide? All of these factors could be triggers for depression and thoughts of suicide.

What you can do

- Be a willing listener – sometimes just knowing that someone cares enough to listen makes a potential suicide feel less isolated and alone. It also puts you in a position where you can suggest avenues of help for your friend or relative, as well as telling other people who might be able to help. For the depressed or suicidal person, it can be hard to see solutions to their problems – talking to someone who listens but doesn't judge can help them find other ways to cope.

- If your friend doesn't come to you to talk, then open the conversation yourself. Sure, it's not easy to talk about suicide – but it's not easy to be left wishing you'd done something after the fact either. Be open, tell the person that you're concerned about them, say they seem depressed and talk a lot about death – are they thinking of suicide?

- Let your friend know they are not alone, that you care about them and want to help them find help. Call the Samaritans helpline and hand them the phone. Go with them to talk to their parents. Be there. And if you're really worried, don't leave that person alone until someone else is there to help, by which I mean someone qualified to take the responsibility of helping your suicidal friend or loved one.

'Be a willing listener – sometimes just knowing that someone cares enough to listen makes a potential suicide feel less isolated and alone.'

If a suicide occurs

Sometimes, despite the support of caring friends and family and the intervention of qualified professionals, someone goes ahead and commits suicide. This brings about a mixture of feelings in the people who care, from guilt that they should have done more to anger that the person has hurt them in this way. Some people are left just too emotionally numb to even feel grief.

Suicide is often considered a selfish gesture, or even an aggressive one.

- One way for survivors to help each other is to break through the barrier of silence and talk about what has happened. Discuss your feelings openly, talk about your friend or loved one, debate why they may have taken their own life.

- It might be difficult at this time, but try to share good memories and celebrate your friend's life. Accept that your friend made a decision – not a good one or one you agree with – but a decision nonetheless. It was a decision made out of pain or desperation and no one is to blame.

- If friends and family agree, perhaps choose a time and hold a ceremony for your friend, giving everyone a chance to talk about their memories and feelings and to say goodbye to the person who has died.

- Feelings of sorrow and grief are normal but if you or another person in your group find those feelings aren't fading, it is responsible to seek some help with a counsellor or doctor, or talk to an older family member if you're in a younger age group, and ask for help.

Summing Up

Society now rightly takes a much more compassionate attitude to suicide and to those who attempt to take their own lives than was the case in the past. Suicide is recognised as the result of deep emotional or physical pain, distress, trauma or mental illness, and it is known that many people who wish to die are suffering from major depression. But suicide and attempted suicide affect not just the person committing the act but their family, friends and colleagues. One person's suicide may trigger similar thoughts in others, particularly those who are already depressed.

There are some indicators that a person is considering suicide but sometimes these aren't understood until too late. They include a pre-occupation with death, giving away treasured belongings, trying to mend old arguments or self-destructive behaviours such as becoming isolated, behaving recklessly, taking drugs or drinking too much alcohol.

There are a number of myths about suicide, such as that someone attempting suicide really wants to die. Frequently, a suicide attempt is a cry for help and in most cases the person can be helped by skilled intervention. People, especially young people, often confide their thoughts of suicide to a friend and ask that it is kept a secret – this is one promise that should always be broken.

If someone confides their intent to end their own life, then it's important that you try to get them to visit their doctor or even the emergency department at your local hospital. Seek help from a parent, teacher or school nurse if you're teenagers, or get in touch with the person's doctor, counsellor or some other health professional. Call the Samaritans or some other helpline on their behalf and hand them the telephone – do whatever you can. Stay with the person and listen while they talk – sometimes a sympathetic listener can defuse a serious situation and convince a suicidal person to seek help. But understand that, while you may do everything you can, a threat of suicide really needs the intervention of a qualified health professional.

And in the final analysis, your friend or loved one may still attempt to take their own life. If that happens, don't play the blame game – understand that you do not have total control over someone else's actions. Survivors can help each other by talking about what has happened and expressing their feelings. This may include a wide range of emotions – from sorrow and numbness to anger that this has happened.

'People, especially young people, often confide their thoughts of suicide to a friend and ask that it is kept a secret – this is one promise that should always be broken.'

Chapter Six

Children Don't Get Depressed, Do They?

We like to think of childhood as a golden time, filled with freedom and love, games and friends. But how many people can honestly say their childhood reflects this idyll? No matter how loving our parents, no matter how well-off or sheltered we are, sometimes bad things happen that a child can't be shielded from. Grandparents – and parents sometimes – die. Parents divorce, families break up, relatives are lost. In bad economic times, jobs are lost and the realities of unemployment, and the stress and uncertainty about the future, will certainly affect children to a greater or lesser degree.

Of course, there are also more terrible things: studies show that as many as one in four children may experience physical or sexual abuse. We read dreadful things in the news every day of abduction, cruelty and abandonment. Our children see these things too. They see violence, war, famine and death on the television and on the Internet.

So it's perhaps a fool's paradise to think that children won't experience depression, but this is what was believed for quite a long time. We know differently now. If you consider that stress is a factor in the triggering of depression, then try to see the world through your child's eyes. Imagine the stress of exam pressure, of trying to be one of the cool crowd at school, of playground bullying and the media-borne expectations to be thin, beautiful and sexy, even for children younger than 10. Remember that children don't have the life experience to put these issues into any kind of perspective. Add to this parental expectations, perhaps family discord, bereavement, divorce, a best friend moving away, a difficult teacher and the whole panorama of world tragedy brought into the living room every evening on the news, and it's easy to see why depression is more than possible for children.

'We like to think of childhood as a golden time, filled with freedom and love, games and friends. But how many people can honestly say their childhood reflects this idyll?'

Signs your child may be depressed:

1) Your normally outgoing child becomes quiet and introverted.

2) They are usually full of energy but now seem listless.

3) They have experienced some family stress, the loss of a parent, close relative or friend or bereavement. Even the death of a loved pet can have a profound effect on a child.

4) You have moved home and your child is missing friends and familiar surroundings.

5) There's a family history of depression.

6) You suspect your child is experiencing bullying at school or in the neighbourhood.

7) Your child's marks at school start to fall or teachers comment that they're inattentive or troublesome in class.

8) Your child loses their appetite – or seems to eat for comfort.

9) They complain that they can't sleep or you can't get them up for school in the morning.

10) They complain about various vague aches and pains, headaches, sore throats, tummy aches, etc.

11) In teenagers, there may be aggressive or reckless behaviour, and acting out.

Studies show that children as young as primary level or even pre-school may experience depression. It's thought that up to 5% of children and teenagers may be suffering from depression at any one point in time. Adolescent girls may be twice as likely to be depressed as adolescent boys. Some speculate that this is because of the pressure placed on girls to look like the models and movie stars they see in the media – and a lot of this may well come from peer pressure. There are a number of studies about the prevalence of depression among children and adolescents. These include reports by the

National Institute for Mental Health in the USA, the World Health Organisation and research papers such as 'Depression and Suicide in Children and Adolescents' - Jellinek and Snyder in *Pediatrics in Review,* 1998, 19: 255-264.

There is also our old friend the 5-HTT gene which increases the possibility of depression in children who inherit the gene from parents who have had the illness.

This list isn't intended as a diagnostic tool. These behaviours may be the result of a number of things, but if your child exhibits one or more of these and they persist for more than a week or so without any change, it's wise to talk to your doctor. They will probably do a physical exam to rule out any underlying health problems before discussing the possibilities of depression.

As you can see, the symptoms of depression in children and teenagers are very like those in adults and the treatments are both similar and equally successful.

If your child has depression

You can help your child recover from depression. No doubt your doctor or counsellor will give you some advice, but the main points would be to ensure that they take any prescribed medication in the right dosages and that you are supportive and non-judgemental. Don't say things like: 'This is just like the way Uncle Bill behaved – and look what happened to him!' or tell your child that you're worried sick over them. They have enough to deal with in getting through whatever has brought about the depression.

Try and see the world through your child's eyes. Did a pet die? It may have been a scruffy old dog, a lazy cat or just a goldfish, but if your child loved it, you can bet that they're grieving for it as intensely as an adult would grieve for a human loved one. Being divorced may be a relief to the parents, but a child may be frightened that they will lose the parent who has moved out, or even believe that their parents have split up because of something they did. Both parents together should talk calmly to the child and explain that the situation isn't their fault, that they still love them but have made the decision to live apart and they'll remain in their life. See *Divorce and Separation – The Essential Guide* (Need2Know) for more information on coping with family separation.

'Being divorced may be a relief to the parents, but a child may be frightened that they will lose the parent who has moved out, or even believe that their parents have split up because of something they did.'

Try to get your child to talk about things that worry them. It may be that they are the victim of a school bully, are having difficulties with a teacher or have had a falling out with their best friend. Failing an important test or not getting an academic prize, not being picked for the sports team and being embarrassed because they aren't developing physically as quickly as other children are all possible causes of their depression. Some children see television coverage of war and violence and become afraid that these things will happen in their town. Sometimes a parent may inadvertently frighten a child by pointing out a news item about a child kidnap or murder and say that that's what happens to children who don't obey their parents. Be aware that your child may take very seriously things that you, as an adult, don't consider to be very important.

What should parents look for?

Childhood depression exhibits signs very like those of depression in older people. The difference is that a child doesn't know what depression is in the way an adult might and is unable to tell you that they feel depressed or even sad. Instead, the first clues you might see may be behavioural changes.

In younger children, depression may manifest itself in naughty behaviour, arguing with parents and siblings or in unusually withdrawn behaviour. Sometimes there are sudden outbursts of violence, such as hitting or biting another child. Often, a child will say they have vague aches and pains like tummy ache, headache or earache, or simply say they feel sick. The child just knows there is something wrong – they don't have the words or the life experience to explain what they feel. The child may also stop playing with friends or going to activities or sports they usually enjoy. You may even get a call from the child's teacher to let you know that their marks are slipping or that a formerly well-behaved child is becoming the class troublemaker. In some cases, depression may also be a warning signal that the child is a victim of sexual abuse.

The symptoms of depression in teenagers are more like those in adults. Teenagers may tell you they are unhappy or that they feel down. They may also be irritable and bad-tempered, withdrawn, untidy and generally hard to live with. Unfortunately, these are behaviours often considered normal for them.

'[Teenagers] may also be irritable and bad-tempered, withdrawn, untidy and generally hard to live with. Unfortunately, these are behaviours often considered normal for them.'

It may take a professional to sort out whether it's depression or not, but a concerned parent should seek professional help. Again, going to your doctor for a physical check-up is probably the best starting place.

Additional warning signs may include:

- Changes in eating and/or sleeping patterns.
- Loss of interest in activities that were formerly enjoyed.
- Loss of energy.
- Low self-esteem, feelings of guilt.
- Inability to concentrate, indecisiveness.
- Difficulty with relationships, social isolation.
- Frequent absences from school, lower marks and test results.
- Moodiness, irritability, rudeness, aggressive behaviour.
- Feelings of hopelessness and helplessness.
- Recurring thoughts of death and suicide, harming oneself.

Schizophrenia – the mood mimic in teenagers

If the mood swings are extreme and the teenager starts to shut themselves in their room, perhaps seems to be talking to themselves or even having hallucinations and gives up bathing and putting on clean clothes, it may be that they're suffering from early onset schizophrenia. Despite the popular belief that this is split personality, schizophrenia is actually an acute form of brain chemical imbalance which, with patience and the proper medication, can be eased.

'At first we put our son's unpleasant behaviour down to the usual teenage moods. He got very anti-social and sometimes wouldn't wash or change his clothes. He caused scenes at home and it got so bad that our daughters refused to come to any family events if he was going to be there. He got into drink and drugs. It's a terrible thing to say about your own son, but we thought he was either crazy or just plain bad. Sometimes we felt like disowning him. He began to threaten suicide and sometimes got violently angry for no apparent reason.

'When we finally found a doctor who diagnosed schizophrenia, it came as a relief. It took some time before they got the balance of drugs right but then Sam was once again the bright, gentle teenager we loved. It was as though some other horrible person had been living in our son's body, and finally we had the boy we loved back again.' Pat. C.

Treatment for children with depression

Children can usually be helped with therapy and some counsellors specialise in working with children and teenagers. The counsellor will work with your child to determine what may have triggered the depressive episode and why the child feels as they do. They will also help the child to bolster their self-esteem and work out a plan to tackle some of the problems that may be causing them to feel bad, such as feeling lonely or unable to do well at school. They will also work on helping the child to overlay negative thoughts with positive ones – a means of developing a more optimistic and confident outlook on the world. This in turn will make the child more relaxed, able to cope and help them to make friends and stand up to bullies.

Because the child doesn't live in the world alone, most therapists will include the parents and siblings in some sessions, encouraging everyone to speak openly about their problems and to find, with the counsellor's guidance, solutions and accommodations that bring them closer together. When a normally happy and confident child becomes depressed, it's hard for other family members to understand what's happening and they too may need some help and counselling.

Antidepressants are sometimes prescribed for children, although many healthcare professionals prefer to try counselling first. This is because some antidepressants do not work as well with children as they might with teenagers or adults. There is also some reluctance to give young children drugs that affect the balance of chemicals in the developing brain.

'I was working really hard at school to get good enough marks to get into university. I had a long term girlfriend who I thought I loved, but suddenly I wondered if I even wanted to be with her – I felt I wasn't good enough for her. Then I was terrified she'd drop me. It felt like there was so much pressure – my parents expected a lot of me because I'd be the first to go on to university if I made it.

'All of a sudden, I was thinking of suicide, of just walking into the sea and it all being over. Fortunately, a friend of my Mum's was a counsellor and I asked her if I could talk to her. She helped me see that there wasn't anything wrong with me, just normal doubts and anxieties, and I learned some relaxation techniques. Most of all, it was good to talk to someone who didn't judge me or tell me to get over it and took me seriously.' Carl J.

Talking to your child about depression

When a child is diagnosed as depressed, it's essential for parents or trusted carers to talk to them and explain what depression is and why it is important for them to take medication or talk to a counsellor. They should make it clear that they love them and that they have nothing to be afraid of.

Talk to your child about their feelings, ask if they feel sad or angry, or if they can describe what's happening inside. Keeping these lines of communication open mean there's a good chance your child will come and talk to you if they need help.

If your child is to go to a family therapist, tell them that it's okay to talk about anything that may be bothering them. Explain that you want them to feel better and that you won't be embarrassed if they say things about the family. Also, explain to your child that going to a therapist isn't a punishment like being sent to the school headteacher; tell them they've not done anything wrong and that the therapist wants to help them find out why they're feeling sad or angry and to help them feel better.

As previously explained, often a counsellor will ask the parents, and sometimes the child's siblings, to attend therapy sessions. Try to get everyone to attend and be as open as possible about family issues. If your child has expressed concern about family dynamics, this is a good place to sort things out. Your child and your whole family will come out of the experience happier.

Explaining a parent's depression to a child

Children can't easily understand what's wrong when one of their parents is depressed. They may feel that Mum's tears or Dad's long silences are because they have done something wrong. Make sure you explain to your child what is happening, that the depression isn't due to anything they have done wrong but is an illness that one of you is trying very hard to get through. Say that everyone can help the parent get better by being kind and patient, so that your child feels empowered rather than helpless.

'I remember being three years old and listening outside a closed door while my mother sobbed and sobbed. She wouldn't come out, she wouldn't talk to me. It was like I didn't exist. In my child's mind, I thought I had done something awful – that I was a terrible person to make my mother cry. It wasn't until many years later that I realised that she was experiencing depression at a time when there was little help or counselling. Now I understand that it wasn't my fault – but that feeling still haunts me. I wish someone had explained it all to me then, I feel it would have made a difference in my own life.' Jean H.

Explaining suicide to a child

It's a fact of life that you can't shield your child or teenager from the experience of a friend or relative committing suicide any more than you can shelter them from the grief of any other sort of bereavement.

But where a child can perhaps understand that a grandparent was very old and has gone to heaven or that a friend or sibling had become very ill and didn't get better, it may be very hard for them to come to terms with someone they care about actually killing themselves.

With young children it's best to keep the explanation short but be open to any questions they may ask. Tell them that the person had become very sad and suffered from an illness called depression. Say that this illness made the person feel they didn't want to live any more but that they weren't thinking straight when this was going on.

You can be a bit more detailed with teenagers and in both instances give the child lots of opportunities to ask questions. Teenagers, in particular, may ask for details of the person's suicide. They're not being ghoulish – it's a way of dealing with what has happened in their own minds.

With both children and teenagers, you can open a debate about suicide and what the person could have done about getting help and getting well from the depression. Let your children know that suicide is not the only or best answer and that anyone feeling that life is not worth living can find help and support.

Explain to your child that feeling sad is normal, especially when there has been a loss or disappointment or when someone is feeling lonely. Say that you are always there to listen if the child has problems or sad feelings and they should come to you. Set an example by talking about your own feelings and the positive steps you take to feel better.

Depression in teenagers

As mentioned earlier, hormonal changes can be a trigger for depression. Add to that all the pressures of adolescence and it's no wonder that some teenagers experience depression.

'But where a child can perhaps understand that a grandparent was very old and has gone to heaven or that a friend or sibling had become very ill and didn't get better, it may be very hard for them to come to terms with someone they care about actually killing themselves.'

They're busy trying to figure out their own place in the world, cope with changing relationships, worrying about whether they are smart enough to make it in the world, concerned as to whether they are one of the cool crowd or disappointed if they're not, being easily embarrassed or humiliated by others and trying to live with the changes taking place in their own bodies. Learning to understand their own sexuality is always an issue during the teenage years, and one fraught with anxiety.

Then there's the pressure, sometimes quite unconscious, from parents who want them to do well at school, mix with the right crowd, get into university or further education and train for a job. It's a lot to ask of anyone, let alone someone just setting out with little life experience to help them keep a perspective.

'Recent studies show that as many as 50% of the teenagers who experience major depression will attempt suicide at least once.'

Some teenagers turn to alcohol or drugs because it may be the done thing in their crowd, or because they see it as a way of coping or even dulling the emotional pain they are experiencing. Perhaps they have seen this example at home when parents smoke or take a few drinks to relax when they're stressed and the teenager sees this as a coping mechanism.

Parents may become so fed up with a teenager's moods that they become critical or angry; or perhaps the parents have troubles of their own and the teen doesn't feel comfortable adding to their burden. For whatever reason, sometimes depression sets in to a point where the young person feels they have no alternatives and nowhere to turn. That's a dangerous time when thoughts of suicide may slip in.

If you suspect your teenage son or daughter is depressed, if you think they may be taking drugs or drinking, or if they exhibit severe mood changes, angry outbursts, shut themselves away or threaten to leave home, these are danger signals that you shouldn't ignore. Recent studies show that as many as 50% of the teenagers who experience major depression will attempt suicide at least once.

Other danger signals are similar to those of adult depression. Don't ignore the symptoms: if your teenager won't talk to you, explain that you are concerned about them and encourage them to see the doctor. Alternatively, suggest visiting the school guidance counsellor, teenage suicide helpline or seeing a counsellor. Try to keep lines of communication open from childhood, and let your teenager know that no matter how bad they may be feeling, there is always help and that you will be there to support them.

Need2Know

Summing Up

Children do get depressed and parents and carers shouldn't ignore some of the symptoms or think it's just a phase and will go away. Because of the possible serious consequences of depression in children, it's probably better to err on the side of caution and seek professional help. The first stop with a child or teenager should always be the family doctor to rule out any possible underlying physical ailment.

Younger children may show depression by becoming withdrawn and moody, failing in school, becoming disruptive, given to temper tantrums or even hitting and biting. They may seem listless and tired, disinterested in their usual activities and shut themselves away from friends. Triggers may include the loss of a loved person or pet, moving house, changing school, family discord or parental separation/divorce, being bullied or having difficulty with a teacher. In some instances, this kind of behaviour can be a warning signal of sexual abuse.

It is important not to just ignore these warning signs in a child or put them down to teenage moods or growing pains. When possible symptoms of depression continue unchanged for more than a week or two, it's time to seek help from a professional. Usually the family doctor will do a physical check-up first to look for any underlying physical illness and then discuss the possibility of depression and the various treatments.

It's hard to shelter children from the difficulties of day-to-day living, from bereavement and family discord, playground bullying, parental divorce, the loss of a much-loved pet, moving to a new neighbourhood, losing a best friend or from the images of violence, war and famine they see each day on the television news or the Internet. Parents should try from early childhood to keep the lines of communication open so that their children know they can turn to Mum or Dad, or another adult relative, to talk about their problems and get an understanding hearing.

'It's hard to shelter children from the difficulties of day-to-day living, from bereavement and family discord, playground bullying or parental divorce.'

Chapter Seven

Depression and Other Serious Health Problems

Not surprisingly, depression is a component of other diseases either as a contributing factor or as a result. It's easy to see that a person suffering a serious illness would feel depressed about their situation, but did you know that there is a link between depression and the onset of some medical conditions?

Depression and obesity – the Catch 22 situation

Recent studies show that there is a link between depression and obesity – and it may not be the obvious one. While it's true that some overweight people may become depressed because they hate the way they look or feel they are socially isolated due to their weight, studies seem to show that in a high percentage of cases, the depression comes first – and is not as a result of being overweight.

In other words, if you're depressed, you may be more likely to be overweight. This appears to be very true in studies which show that children and adolescents who are depressed may grow up into obese adults.

Much of the current research centres on something called the HPA axis, a hormonal pathway in the brain which is linked to obesity, behavioural problems and depression in children.

One theory is that someone who is depressed may take to eating larger amounts than normal in an unconscious bid to boost low serotonin levels, which are also considered to be a cause of depression. In other words, they may be trying to eat their way out of depression.

Unfortunately, this is more likely to lead to the weight gain observed in some depressed patients and therefore to a downward spiral of depression and overeating. Remember that being seriously overweight carries its own health risks.

The good news is that researchers are looking into the effects of antidepressant SSRIs because making the person's serotonin uptake more effective may remove the need to overeat. If you are depressed and overweight, this may be something to talk over with your doctor.

Depression and stress

According to research from the Mayo Clinic, chronic stress can create depression – probably not a big surprise to anyone suffering from trauma-triggered stress. Everyone has their own way of responding to stress; events that may trigger major anxiety in some people seem to roll off others like water off a duck's back. There doesn't seem to be any decisive reason for this, except that some people are more vulnerable to stress than others. Also, some of us can learn from our parents and older relatives ways of coping that allow us to keep stress in perspective.

As with depression, relaxation techniques such as deep breathing, yoga, meditation and massage therapies can be a big help. Stress can be alleviated by taking care of yourself – eat nutritious food, get some exercise every day or as often as you can, make sure you get enough sleep and avoid using alcohol or other addictive substances. It's well known that some people turn to drink or drugs as a means of alleviating stress – again, this is often a learned behaviour – but in the long run, alcohol, tobacco and illegal drugs mask the stress rather than clearing it up. It's better to deal with problems than try to drown them. For more information on stress, see Stress – The Essential Guide (Need2Know).

'Stress can be alleviated by taking care of yourself – eat nutritious food, get some exercise every day or as often as you can, make sure you get enough sleep and avoid using alcohol or other addictive substances.'

Depression and eating disorders

It seems that only in relatively recent years have eating disorders been recognised. Whether this is because bulimia and anorexia are increasing at a rate that has made them recognised as illnesses in themselves, or whether it is because they are a relatively new phenomenon, is open for discussion.

Bulimia involves eating large amounts of food in binges and then purging by inducing vomiting or by the use of laxatives. Anorexics starve themselves voluntarily to the point of emaciation and will find all sorts of excuses to avoid situations involving food, including family meal times. In both conditions, the sufferers still see themselves as looking fat despite sometimes massive weight loss. The starvation and lack of nutrition can lead to serious health complications and even death, and sufferers need medical intervention as soon as possible.

There has probably always been some manifestation of eating disorders, and modern day pressures to have a model-thin appearance may have contributed to their growth. Certainly, in times when there wasn't such an abundance of food, there was probably little problem with overeating and purging through vomiting or laxatives among working people.

'Much of the current research centres on something called the HPA axis, a hormonal pathway in the brain which is linked to obesity, behavioural problems and depression in children.'

While it is known that some depressed people may overeat in an unconscious bid to raise their serotonin levels and in turn elevate their mood, it is also known that certain eating disorders seem to be linked to depression in a chicken-and-egg way. Whether the depression follows the emotional problems and physical deprivation of the eating disorder, or whether the eating disorder arises from the depression, is still a subject for lively debate.

Therefore, be aware that there can be a link between eating disorders – including overeating, compulsive eating, bulimia and anorexia – and depression. Talk to your doctor if you fear you or someone you care about is engaged in these practices.

Alcoholism, drug abuse and depression

While no studies so far have shown that alcoholism actually causes depression, they have a number of symptoms in common. One is that people often drink to excess in order to control sadness or other emotional pain, or to cope with a personal trauma. It is believed that 30-50% of alcoholics also suffer from depression. Although alcohol makes you feel better when you first have a drink or two, the good mood doesn't last because alcohol can actually spark depressed feelings in the let-down which follows the alcohol high.

Many alcoholics who try to quit drinking find it hard because depression usually sets in when they first withdraw from alcohol, making the craving for a drink 'to take off the edge' much stronger and harder to resist. Also, if you are depressed and start drinking heavily, the chances of suicidal thoughts intensify as the alcohol lessens inhibitions and puts you at greater risk of suicide. Alcohol has the effect of impairing your judgement while increasing the likelihood of impetuous or reckless behaviour. This may lead to driving while impaired by alcohol or drugs, or deliberately driving recklessly in an attempt to commit suicide. Alcoholics are also known for drug overdoses.

See *Alcoholism – The Family Guide* (Need2Know) for more information on alcohol and drinking.

Symptoms linking alcoholism and depression

- A family history of depression or alcoholism puts you at higher risk of developing either health problem.

- Alcohol can intensify the feeling of depression.

- If you are depressed, drinking alcohol may cause a relapse in your condition.

- If you are an alcoholic with a history of depression, you should talk to your doctor or healthcare professional about close monitoring when you are in the early stages of withdrawal.

- Alcohol can reduce the symptoms of depression over the space of three or four weeks drinking time, but those symptoms return even stronger when the alcohol intake stops.

If you (or a friend) are depressed and drinking heavily, it is important that you seek medical attention because of the heightened suicide risks.

Other conditions

Huntingdon's disease

Huntingdon's disease is an inherited condition caused by an abnormal gene. It produces uncontrolled movements, loss of intellectual faculties and emotional disturbance.

Depression, mood swings and irritability are among the early warning symptoms of Huntingdon's disease, along with perceptual problems that lead to difficulties driving and learning new things and a deterioration in memory and decision-making skills.

Schizophrenia

People with schizophrenia often experience depression as well which increases their level of suffering from this illness. It also increases the possibility of suicide attempts. It is not fully understood why the two illnesses occur together but it's probably not coincidental. Possibly depression is a result of the uncontrolled moods of schizophrenia.

It is also possible that the physical neglect that is often part of schizophrenics' lifestyle can result in the person getting run-down physically and becoming depressed. Sometimes the medications used to treat schizophrenic symptoms may also lead to depression as a side effect. Schizophrenics may also use illicit drugs or alcohol to relieve their symptoms and these can be depression triggers.

As you can see, the co-relation of depression and schizophrenia is a complex and tangled one. There is no doubt, however, that when a doctor considers the onset of depression in a patient diagnosed with schizophrenia, they will look at lifestyle, physical health, medications and other factors before setting a course of treatment.

Anxiety conditions and depression

There are a number of anxiety disorders, some of them include phobias such as obsessive compulsive disorder, post traumatic stress disorder, social phobia, separation anxiety and hypochondria.

According to a 2005 survey, about 58% of people diagnosed with depression also suffered from some form of anxiety. GAD – generalised anxiety disorder – is more common in women than men.

GAD is a catch-all title for serious anxiety difficulties that don't result from other individual anxiety disorders such as separation anxiety or social phobia, each of which stem from a specific fear. People with GAD experience uncontrollable anxiety about everyday events to the extent that it interferes with their day-to-day lives. While they may worry, like the rest of us perhaps, about work, money and their families, they also get overly anxious about relatively minor matters like being organised, keeping their homes tidy and having projects finished on time. Because of this, young people with GAD often fail to reach their potential in school and in their early careers, and are more likely to get involved with substance abuse and to develop other mental health issues.

Symptoms of GAD

You may be experiencing GAD if:

- You get extremely anxious and worried about relatively ordinary events, such as a school test or work review, with the anxiety frame of mind going on for months.

- You can't control the amount of worrying you do and you worry excessively about relatively minor things.

- You worry to the point where it interferes with your social life, work and relationships.

- You feel restless and tense most of the time.

- You get tired easily.

- Your muscles are tense and you have difficulty concentrating.

- You find it hard to get to sleep, or when you do sleep you are restless, perhaps with disturbing dreams.

Again, this list is not intended as a diagnostic tool. Only your health care professional can offer you a proper diagnosis after consideration of symptoms, background, lifestyle and a physical check-up.

Anxiety disorders are treatable, usually with counselling therapy to help you relearn your thinking into positive, rather than negative, thoughts and learning to keep a balanced perception of events. Talk to your doctor or a counsellor for help.

Psychotic depression

This is an extreme form of depression, characterised by hallucinations, hearing voices, erratic behaviour and paranoid tendencies. While this sounds very like schizophrenia, people with psychotic tendencies are generally painfully aware that the things they see may not be there and words whispered in their ears may come from voices that don't exist.

Because they realise that these things are not real, and because they realise that talking about them may make them sound crazy, psychotic depressives tend to be ashamed and usually try to hide the condition. This not only makes it hard to diagnose but means that the symptoms may worsen to a point where they can no longer be hidden before they are noticed by other people, meaning that the person goes untreated for too long a time. This increases the risk of bipolar depression, relapses of psychotic depression and suicide.

This rather frightening sounding type of depression is not particularly rare: approximately 25% of people who are admitted to hospital because of depression are suffering from the symptoms of psychotic depression.

The exact cause of this illness isn't yet known but it appears from recent research that hormonal imbalances, previous bipolar depression and a family history are all factors. The hormone imbalance factor can lead to psychotic depression being an offshoot of post-partum depression, as new mothers experience fluctuations of hormones after childbirth (see chapter 1).

Psychotic depression is characterised by:

- Extreme anxiety and distress.
- Disturbed sleep, often with frightening nightmares.
- Hallucinations.
- Delusions and the sense of not being able to control your own thoughts.
- Anxiety disorders.
- Symptoms of paranoia and hypochondria.

Hypochondria and depression

Hypochondria, or hypocondriasis as it is sometimes called, is an anxiety disorder. Hypochondriacs focus on their own physical condition, seeing symptoms of many different illnesses in every sneeze and muscle twitch. They are very difficult to convince that they are in good health and sometimes doctors become impatient, as do family and friends. Sadly, there's an old saying, 'just because you're paranoid doesn't mean to say they aren't after you', and this can be applied to hypochondria too. In the plethora of symptoms hypochondriacs claim to have, a genuine illness could be missed.

Such worry about physical illness can trigger anxiety attacks. As you can imagine, this condition prevents the person from enjoying a normal life and puts strains on their relationships with other people and medical professionals. They constantly seek reassurance that they're not seriously ill, while at the same time coming up with new symptoms to counter any arguments that they are well.

Common symptoms of hypochondria:

- Irrational belief that the person has a serious illness.
- Fear of dying through illness.
- Inability to accept a doctor's diagnosis.
- Constant checking out oneself for physical changes that might indicate illness.
- Diagnosing one's own symptoms, usually misinterpreting them.

- Complaints of numerous vague aches and pains that change over short periods of time.

While it has been the subject for humour columnists' jokes, hypochondria can have serious consequences, leading to depression, anxiety attacks, loss of appetite, no interest in sex, loss of interest in social life or other activities, self-consciousness and a lack of motivation.

Hypochondria can be triggered in some cases by the long illness or death of a loved one or friend, increased personal stress, a very real fear of an illness which grows out of proportion and by ill health in childhood.

It can be treated with hypnotherapy, cognitive behaviour counselling therapy and, in some instances, antidepressant medication.

Post traumatic stress disorder

Post traumatic stress disorder (PTSD) is something that has been brought to public attention a great deal due to the suffering of soldiers returning from the various wars and peacekeeping missions. It is accepted now that for many people, the experience and the trauma of war – being fired upon, being injured or seeing friends injured or killed – can trigger PTSD. During the First World War there is evidence that a number of young men were executed as cowards or deserters when in fact they were actually suffering from this mental illness and were unable to control their behaviour.

Thousands of British troops may have been diagnosed with PTSD. According to the Ministry of Defence, as early as 2006 about 1.5% of military personnel had to be evacuated from Iraq with 'serious psychiatric problems'. An estimated 40,000 US military personnel have been diagnosed with PTSD since 2003, and it's expected that figure will increase by 50% in the next few years. Experts believe that the figure may actually be considerably higher – some soldiers are reluctant to admit to having problems, such as flashbacks of painful memories, feelings of isolation or loss of control, etc, because they are either ashamed or they are afraid that being diagnosed with PTSD will affect their military careers.

PTSD is usually triggered by a sudden life threatening event (being under fire during war, experiencing a major natural disaster or a severe car accident for example) where you experience intense fear and a sense of horror or helplessness. It is described as 'a normal reaction to an abnormal situation, a deeply shocking or disturbing experience' by Harley Street stress consultant David Reeves in an article on PTSD published on the Mindtech Association website. It can involve sleeplessness, anxiety attacks, difficulty concentrating, flashbacks, loss of control and sometimes even violent outbursts due to disorientation. For a diagnosis of PTSD, the symptoms are usually expected to be present for longer than three months.

About 80% of people diagnosed with PTSD also suffer from another identifiable mental health component such as depression, generalised anxiety disorder, panic disorder or alcohol/drug abuse. PTSD usually results from the experience of a life threatening trauma, or one that is perceived as life threatening. It can be very hard to diagnose because it is so like depression or an anxiety disorder, but the recent trauma is a key factor. The effects can be reduced by intervention as soon as is feasible after the traumatic event, called structured stress debriefings, to help the person cope and come to terms with the experience.

Because there are a number of disorders that can co-exist with PTSD, it's important that they are all treated simultaneously. Treatment usually involves antidepressant drugs, psychotherapy, counselling and education to help the patient understand what is happening.

Summing Up

Depression has a chicken-and-egg relationship with a number of other illnesses, as it's not fully known whether the other illness occurred because of the depression or whether the depression grew from the illness. We can understand that someone with a serious medical condition may feel depressed about their circumstances, and a survivor of war, natural disaster or major car crash might well feel depressed for some time afterwards as they recover. It's easy to see why the stress of a battle situation where military personnel have their lives in jeopardy, see friends killed or maimed or must take the life of another human being could trigger PTSD.

Likewise, depression stemming from stress or as part of general anxiety disorder is easy to understand, but it's harder to grasp the connection between eating disorders or hypochondria and depression. However, research has shown that links do exist and future discoveries could show that depression plays a role in many other health issues and may explain why.

There are a number of mental illnesses that contain a depressive element, and some that lead to depression and vice versa. Again, anyone who thinks they may have depression should make sure they visit their doctor for a physical check up, as depressive symptoms can be part of many underlying physical ailments. These illnesses include hypothyroid (underactive thyroid gland), diabetes, chronic fatigue syndrome and multiple sclerosis.

Chapter Eight

Life After Depression – Looking Forward

When someone is in the throes of depression, the future may seem like a strange concept. It's hard to look ahead when you're struggling to just get through the next hour, the next day. But the depression will lift and there will come a day when you feel yourself again and want to get on with your life. You may even feel an imperative to get extra fulfilment from your work and personal life because you feel you've missed out while being sunk in depression.

But then that awful thought crops up: what if I get depressed again?

'After a few months seeing a counsellor and working out some of the issues that had got me down, I started to feel really well. At last I'd dropped the burden of the things that haunted me from childhood. I was free to get on with my life. I stopped seeing the counsellor, but without his support life seemed to get on top of me again. I didn't want to confide in my family because I thought they'd be disappointed in me. I felt like a weak person who couldn't cope with life. I was depressed again. With the help of my counsellor, I pulled out of it but now I'm afraid that this is going to be my life, lurching from one depression to another. Is there anything I can do to help myself?' Peter P.

The future

Some people do not experience a recurrence of depression but many do. Statistics show that one in three people who have had depression will experience another episode within a year; 50-80% will have another episode of depression within their lifetime. Some people experience more frequent and longer bouts of depression as they get older.

Sometimes the reason for a relapse is simple: either the patient was not on a long enough course of antidepressants or the failure to include psychotherapy counselling led to serious unresolved issues triggering further depressions.

What can you do?

To begin with you can recognise that relapses do occur, that it's not your fault and that you survived your first episode of depression and you can survive another. It won't be fun, but you now know what to expect and you know to seek help. It's very important that you don't beat yourself up or play the blame game if you do get depressed. Recognise that you have done everything you can to avoid this and now you'll do everything you can to get through it. Don't feel helpless – you are empowered because you have things that you can do to recover from this depression.

The easy stuff

If you are put on antidepressants, make sure you take them exactly as prescribed and only stop taking them on your doctor's orders. Sometimes people start to feel better and decide to quit with the medication before it has run its course – this can lead to a further episode of depression.

If you are depressed, consider seeing a counsellor to discover if there are personal issues that trigger your bad feelings. Many counsellors will suggest going on a maintenance programme rather than quitting counselling 'cold turkey'. This means that you will continue to see your counsellor, but less and less frequently until the visits stop altogether. This allows you to discuss any further anxieties that come up over time even though you are feeling better, and the support the counsellor is able to give helps you remain well. Your counsellor can also help you to identify the triggers that may cause you to feel depressed and help you learn to control them.

The harder stuff

Here are some things that you can do by yourself, although don't hesitate to seek the help of your doctor or counsellor if you need it. You will probably notice that there are some warning signs that you are becoming depressed; perhaps you are more tired than usual, lethargic and less interested in things you normally enjoy. You may find that your thoughts are becoming very negative and your view of the world and your own hopes for the future are dimmed.

This is where you should remember the effects of positive thinking, of overlaying negative thoughts about yourself and your situation with positive ones. Use the deep breathing and relaxation exercises that your counsellor or health professional taught you. Consider taking a holiday or even a day trip somewhere you want to visit. A change of scene can be revitalising. Get together with upbeat people for a relaxing chat or an outing. Make sure your diet has lots of fresh fruit and vegetables, check your caffeine and alcohol intake and make sure you are getting out and about for activities in the fresh air and sunshine.

These are all things that should lift your mood and should be part of your daily regimen – your own Plan A for avoiding depression.

Sometimes there is a recognisable trigger that sparks depression. Some of these are triggers that you can control – others are triggers that you can't do anything about. Learn to accept and understand the difference rather than feel bad because you let something get you down which, in reality, you were unable to do anything about.

Triggers you can control

You can learn to avoid or resolve some of these triggers:

- Lack of good nutrition.

- Not getting enough exercise, sleep and relaxation.
- Family conflict.
- Being bullied at work.
- Stress caused by overwork or being unhappy at work.
- Long commuting times.
- Not taking a break or 'me' time.
- Drinking alcohol, smoking or the use of illegal drugs.

The triggers in the list above are all things you can do something about. Learn to eat a well-balanced diet, avoid alcohol, exercise regularly and make sure you get enough sleep. Do your relaxation exercises and get out and do things that you enjoy. These should be social activities as well as some of the solitary hobbies you may like. If there is family conflict, identify the source and causes. If there's always a fight at a get-together, try to talk to the people involved beforehand and settle the matter – or else politely decline the invitation and give your reasons.

Are you being bullied at work? You'd be surprised how many adults report that they are bullied at work, and the result can be lost work time, depression and even suicide. According to the Andrea Adams Trust, a non-profit charity focussing on bullying in the workplace, at least 40% of UK organisations don't have an effective policy in place to handle bullying.

> At least one in four people will be bullied at some point during their working lives. According to www.banbullyingatwork.com, 18.9 million working days are lost each year to industry as a direct result of workplace bullying, costing the UK economy 6 billion pounds and massively impacting on productivity, creativity, morale and general employee wellbeing.

But there are solutions:

- Talk to your supervisor or manager – or if they are the ones doing the bullying, go higher. Talk to the human resources office. Ask for a conflict negotiation. Take it to your union representative, if you have one. If it continues, get the advice of a solicitor. If the situation is unsalvageable, then look for another job – a difficult project, perhaps, in hard economic times but worth it to save yourself from repeated episodes of depression.

■ The same holds true if you are overworked or unhappy in your job. Talk to the higher ups and your co-workers to see what can be done to redistribute the workload or make the general work ambience more pleasant and more interesting.

■ Long commuting times: if changing to a job nearer home isn't an option, or if you love your work, consider taking along a good book, a computer game, your MP3 player or a notebook and see what you can do to make the travel time more productive or enjoyable.

■ Take any holidays that are owed to you and use them. Do something you enjoy – it doesn't have to cost the earth. Doing something relaxing, preferably in a change of scenery, can be quite a refreshing boost.

■ As for problems caused by alcohol, smoking or illegal drugs – you have the remedy in your own hands. If you cannot give up by yourself, seek help from your doctor or a quit smoking/drinking/drug addiction programme that you can find through your local health unit or wellness clinic.

■ Take control of the things you can control.

Triggers you may not be able to avoid or control

These are some of the events that are stressful and potential depression triggers which you may need to seek help and support in coping with if they occur:

■ Bereavement.

■ Divorce.

■ Unemployment.

■ Serious illness (your own or that of a loved one).

■ Financial difficulties.

- Accidents.

- Starting a new job.

- Moving house.

Learn to understand that some events and situations cannot be avoided and some don't even give you any warning before they occur. When dealing with one of these, it's helpful to sit down and list the problems, how you feel and what you can actually do about it. A to-do list can be a great help in coping with many of these triggers because it gives you a sense of being in control. It may help to have a loved one or close friend sit down with you to discuss the problems and how you can cope. Doing this may offer an opportunity for the two of you to grow closer and develop a mutually supportive relationship.

Another survival method suggested by therapists is to keep a journal in which you write down your feelings and the associated events each day. No need for a great literary work – this is just a record of events versus depressed mood and a therapeutic way for you to get your thoughts and feelings in order. Many people report feeling lighter after writing down the things that have been bothering them. A tip, though: if your writing contains angry or derogatory remarks about your nearest and dearest, make sure you destroy the pages or keep them in a safe place. Having the target of your ill feelings accidentally read about it can ruin an otherwise healthy relationship!

Consider having a Plan A and a Plan B. Plan A is your daily routine that you can follow when things are going smoothly, keeping to a good diet and exercise plan, recognising possible triggers and acting to minimise their impact.

Plan B is for those days when you simply don't want to get out of bed in the morning, the days when depression creeps up and you don't care what happens. This is when you most need a support system: a friend you can call who'll drop by to visit or meet you out for coffee or a walk and a chat, a supportive therapy group with other people who experience depression or some similar plan that will get you moving. If there's no group near you – and your local health unit or doctor's office should know – then consider starting your own. You may be surprised how many people would appreciate a buddy system for those borderline depressed days.

But the moment you feel that you really are becoming depressed, get help.

Six things you can do to help someone who's depressed

1) Be patient – remember they didn't choose to be depressed.

2) Talk to them about what's going on or be prepared to be silent and listen.

3) Stay in contact with them – phone, email, send a card. Don't let them become isolated. When someone is depressed they may not be the best company, but that's when they most need you.

4) Be encouraging, find something about them to praise and bite back any criticisms.

5) Support them by learning about local services that are available for people with depression and offer to go along with them for their first meeting to give moral support.

6) Be aware of any mood changes or worsening of the depression and encourage your friend or loved one to go to the doctor or contact a health professional.

When should you stop the medication or counselling?

Antidepressants usually take weeks to show their effectiveness, so be patient and take your pills as directed. At the other extreme, sometimes people feel really well again and stop taking their medication without consulting their doctor. Never do this – it takes time to get those brain chemicals back in balance, and just because you're feeling better doesn't mean that the job is done. As already explained, take medication as your doctor advises and always consult them before you stop taking it.

If you have been in counselling, the same rule applies: you may feel that you've got a handle on the issues that triggered your depression and you're feeling good. But if you stop counselling before you're really ready, you may be throwing away the regular support that your counsellor provides and this could lead to slipping back into depression.

Some counsellors recommend a short, intensive series of visits, others prefer to work more slowly. Either way, stopping cold turkey in your counselling can be as bad as stopping cold turkey with medication. Most counsellors will recommend a gradual weaning away from your regular visits and put you on a maintenance programme where your appointments will be less and less frequent until they stop altogether. This gives you time to venture out into the world and see if your depression is truly at bay while you know you still have the support of your counsellor just a telephone call away.

Six things you can do for yourself

1) Don't set overly ambitious goals just because you're feeling better – give yourself time to get back on form.

2) When faced with a big project or a major depression trigger, try to list the step-by-step actions you need to take so that you feel in control.

3) Enlist the help and support of your family, friends and co-workers.

4) Set up support systems so you always have a reason to get out of bed in the morning and there's an understanding friend or a therapy group buddy that you can talk to.

5) Take care of yourself, make sure you sleep enough, eat well, exercise and relax both on your own and socially.

6) Think positively. Try to overlay negative thoughts with positive ones.

Can you add your own antidepressant stand-bys to this list? Are there things you do that make you feel better?

Summing Up

The spectre of relapse for anyone who has experienced an episode of depression is very real. Given the bad effects of depression and the way everything, especially decision making and planning, can become too much bother, it's a good idea to think of contingency plans before you become depressed again. It's a bit like the old Plan A and Plan B: set up your support system and resources so that when you feel that dull sense of depression creeping in, you can man the barricades and set about staving it off.

For people in a relationship with someone with depression, this could be an opportunity for the two of you to renew your relationship on a stronger footing and a chance to develop a closer lifestyle by working together to identify and resolve depression triggers.

When faced with one of these depression triggers, learn when you can avoid them or what you can do to resolve or control the problem. When there is an event – such as a family get-together or staff meeting that you know will be argumentative – try to deal with personal differences before the event. Finally, know when you need to seek outside help and support from your medical doctor or your counsellor.

Help List

Emergency helplines

These are numbers you can call to speak to a counsellor if you are in crisis or suicidal. Another alternative is to go to your local hospital's emergency room and explain your situation to a doctor or nurse there.

The Association for Post Natal Illness

145 Dawes Road, Fulham, London, SW6 7EB
Tel: 0207 386 0868
www.apni.org
Support for mothers suffering post natal illness. Also aims to raise public awareness of the illness and to encourage research. Email contact form on site. For urgent help outside office hours, please call Parentline or The Samaritans.

ChildLine

NSPCC, Weston House, 42 Curtain Road, London, EC2A 3NH
Tel: 0800 1111 (helpline for children)
0808 800 5000 (helpline for adults through NSPCC)
www.childline.org.uk
Childline is a free helpline for children and young people in the UK to talk about their problems. In England the service is provided by the NSPCC and in Scotland by Children 1st, on the NSPCC's behalf. The service is confidential and children can talk about any problem, including bullying, abuse, gangs, pregnancy, drugs, depression and running away from home.

Crime Victims Helpline

Tel: 1850 211407 (helpline)
info@crimevictimshelpline.ie
Support for victims and witnesses of crime in the Republic of Ireland. For UK see Victim Support.

National Drugs Helpline

Tel: 0800 77 66 00 (helpline)

www.talktofrank.com

A 24 hour, free and confidential helpline for people addicted to drugs and their families. Available seven days a week. Email contact form on site.

Parentline Plus

520 Highgate Studios, 53-79 Highgate Road, Kentish Town, London, NW5 1TL

Tel: 0808 800 2222 (helpline)

www.parentlineplus.org.uk

National charity working with and for parents. As well as the support helpline, this organisation offers support groups, workshops, local services and training. Email contact form on site.

Samaritans

Chris, PO Box 9090, Stirling, FK8 2SA

Tel: 084 57 909090 (helpline)

1850 609090 (helpline Ireland)

jo@samaritans.org

www.samaritans.org

Samaritans provides a confidential support service for people who are depressed, feeling distressed or considering suicide. The service is available 24 hours a day in the UK and Ireland.

Victim Support

England and Wales: Victim Support National Centre, Hallam House, 56-60 Hallam Street, London, W1W 6JL

Tel: 0845 303 0900 (helpline)

www.victimsupport.org.uk

Scotland: 15/23 Hardwell Close, Edinburgh, EH8 9RX

Tel: 0845 6039 213 (helpline)

info@victimsupportsco.org.uk

Northern Ireland: 3rd floor, Annsgate House, 70-74 Ann Street, Belfast, BT1 4EH

Tel: 0845 303 0900 (helpline)

info@victimsupportni.org.uk

Support for victims of crime. You can use the Supportline by mail by writing to: Hannibal House, Elephant and Castle Shopping Centre, London, SE1 6TB. Outside office hours call the Samaritans. For Republic of Ireland see Crime Victims Helpline.

Women's Aid

Women's Aid Federation of England, Head Office, PO Box 391, Bristol, BS99 7WS
Tel: 0808 2000 247 (helpline)
helpline@womensaid.org.uk
www.womensaid.org.uk
24 hour national helpline on domestic violence. Provides help and information for women experiencing domestic violence or sexual abuse.

Youthline

YouthLine Ltd, The Lodge, Coopers Hill, Bagshot Road, Bracknell, Berkshire, RG12 7QS
Tel: 01344 311200
info@youthlineuk.com
www.youthlinecounselling.co.uk
Provides confidential, free counselling to young people in Berkshire about bullying, drugs, etc, as well as counselling for children aged eight to 11 and their families. There are also two text numbers, 07963 779007 and, for bullying, 07963 779003.

Resources

The following is a list of resources with information about organisations helping with depression and some of its attendant problems.

About.com: Pediatrics

www.pediatrics.about.com
American site including information about depression in children.

Action on Addiction

Head Office, East Knoyle, Salisbury, Wiltshire, SP3 6BE
Tel: 0845 1264130 (helpline)
www.actiononaddiction.org.uk
Charity to help all those affected by addictions, including research and family support.

Addaction

67-69 Cowcross Street, London, EC1M 6PU
Tel: 020 7251 5860
www.addaction.org.uk
This charity's website gives information and help for people addicted to alcohol or drugs.

Al-Anon

England and Wales (main office): 61 Great Dover Street, London, SE1 4YF
Tel: 020 7403 0888 (helpline 10.00am-10.00pm, 365 days a year)
enquiries@al-anonuk.org.uk
Scotland: Al-Anon Information Centre, Mansfield Park Building, Unit 6, 22 Mansfield Street, Partick, Glasgow, G11 5QP
Tel: 0141 339 8884 (helpline 10.00am-10.00pm, 365 days a year)
Northern Ireland: Al-Anon Information Centre, Peace House, 224 Lisburn Road, Belfast, BT9 6GE
Tel: 028 9068 2368 (helpline 10.00am-1.00pm, Monday-Friday; 6.00pm-11.00pm seven days a week)
Republic of Ireland: Al-Anon Information Centre, Room 5, 5 Capel Street, Dublin 1, Republic of Ireland
Tel: 01 873 2699 (helpline 10.30am-2.30 pm, Monday-Friday)
www.al-anonuk.org.uk
Aimed at the families and friends of alcoholics and people trying to give up drinking, offering support groups and meetings.

Alcoholics Anonymous

PO Box 1, 10 Toft Green, York, YO1 7ND
Tel: 0845 769 7555 (helpline)
www.alcoholics-anonymous.org.uk

A support organisation with offices throughout the world. Organises support groups and meetings for people trying to give up drinking alcohol. See the website for more information and to find a group near you. Alcoholics Anonymous does not charge fees or have religious or political affiliations.

Alcoholics Anonymous Ireland

General Service Office, Unit 2, Block C, Santry Business Park, Swords Road, Dublin 9, Republic of Ireland
Tel: 353 18420700
gso@alcoholicsanonymous.ie
www.alcoholicsanonymous.ie
Alcoholics Anonymous in the Republic of Ireland. 'Our primary purpose is to stay sober and help other alcoholics to achieve sobriety.'

Andrea Adams Trust

Hova House, 1 Hova Villas, Hove, East Sussex, BN3 3DH
Tel: 01273 704 900 (helpline)
www.andreaadamstrust.org
A non-profit charity focused on tackling bullying in the workplace. Email using contact form on site.

BBC Health

www.bbc.co.uk/health/womens_health/mind_depression.shtml
See the BBC Health website pages for information on depression and seasonal affective disorder (SAD).

Bipolar Aware

info@bipolaraware.co.uk
www.bipolaraware.co.uk
A 'family guide' to bipolar disorder. This self help website contains information about diagnosis, treatments, education, etc. It also has forums and anecdotal material. The site was established by Mark Hannant to help others with this illness. He experienced bipolar disorder himself but states he is not a medical or mental health professional.

The Black Dog

www.theblackdog.net
An Irish site specifically for men which provides information on psychological health. Chatroom and discussion groups. On site email form.

CombatStress

The chief executive, Combat Stress, Tyrwhitt House, Oaklawn Road, Leatherhead, Surrey, KT22 0BX
Tel: 01372 841 600
contactus@combatstress.org.uk
www.combatstress.org.uk
Supports discharged members of the military and merchant navy experiencing mental health problems, including post traumatic stress disorder, with a regional network of welfare officers available to visit at home or in hospital.

Depression Alliance

212 Spitfire Studios, 63-71 Collier Street, London, N1 9BE
information@depressionalliance.org
www.depressionalliance.org
Provides information and support services as well as a network of self help groups. Please email this address if you have any queries about the supporter scheme: supporters@depressionalliance.org.

Ealing Kids Anti-Bullying Strategy – Children's and Young People's Version

www.ealingkids.org/_files/plan/bullying.pdf
A lovely site with input, visual and written, by children from Blair Peach Primary School and others talking about bullying. The site also contains a good selection of helpline contact numbers and sites for other organisations.

GROW

Tel: 1890 474474 (infoline)
info@grow.ie
www.grow.ie

An Irish support group of people who suffer or have suffered from mental illness. They have local groups in many areas. GROW is a mental health organisation supporting people who have suffered or are suffering from mental health problems. They have a special '12-step' programme.

Health.com

www.health.com/depression
Interesting site with many pages of information and advice for those experiencing depression and their families.

Internet Mental Health

www.mentalhealth.com
This is an American site with a wealth of information about health issues, including mental health and depression, cyclothymic disorder and other depression-related illnesses. Follow the link marked 'Disorders'.

Kidscape

2 Grosvenor Gardens, London, SW1W 0DH
Tel: 08451 205 204 (helpline)
020 7730 3300 (office)
www.kidscape.org.uk
Kidscape is committed to keeping children safe from abuse. It is the first charity in the UK established specifically to prevent bullying and child sexual abuse. Kidscape believes that protecting children from harm is key. They advise that children experiencing bullying should contact Childline. Email resources on the website.

Medical Foundation for the Care of Victims of Torture

Medical Foundation London, 111 Isledon Road, Islington, London, N7 7JW
Tel: 020 7697 7777
www.torturecare.org.uk
Medical, social and psychotherapeutic help and support for victims of torture. Site has news, facts and survivor stories as well as a treatment referral facility. Also has offices in North East and North West England and Scotland – contact details available on main website contact page. Also email form on website.

Medicinenet

www.medicinenet.com
American site with a lot of information about depression and related illnesses.

Mind (National Association for Mental Health)

England: 15-19 Broadway, London, E15 4BQ
Wales: 3rd Floor, Quebec House, Castlebridge, 5-19 Cowbridge Road East, Cardiff, CF11 9AB
Tel: 0845 766 0163 (infoline)
contact@mind.org.uk
www.mind.org.uk
Provides services throughout England and Wales for people with mental health problems, and campaigns for better treatment, patients' rights and better medical practices.

Narcotics Anonymous

202 City Road, London, EC1V 2PH
Tel: 0845 3733366 or 020 77300009 (helplines)
ukso@ukna.org
www.ukna.org
Website for England, Scotland and Wales; helpline numbers for other countries are available on the site. This organisation is a voluntary community of people who have a drug problem and want to get help, regardless of what drug or combination of drugs have been used, and irrespective of age, sex, religion, race, creed or class. According to the website, the only requirement for membership is a desire to stop using drugs.

Narcotics Anonymous Ireland

PO Box 1368, Cardiff Lane, Dublin 2, Republic of Ireland
www.na-ireland.org
Irish branch of Narcotics Anonymous (see above). Helpline numbers for four areas and online email form given on site.

National Self-Harm Network

NSHN, PO Box 7264, Nottingham, NG1 6WJ

nshncg@hotmail.co.uk
www.nshn.co.uk
Support for self-harmers and their families. This site also campaigns for better understanding of this illness.

Northern Ireland Association for Mental Health (NIAMH)

Central Office, 80 University Street, Belfast, BT7 1HE
Tel: 028 9032 8474
alisondeane@niamh.co.uk
www.niamh.co.uk
Provides local support and aims to raise awareness of mental health issues. Support services across Northern Ireland includes housing schemes, home support, advocacy and research as well as public education and information.

Northern Ireland Centre for Trauma and Transformation

2 Retreat Close, Killyclogher Road, Omagh, Co. Tyrone, Northern Ireland, BT79 0HW
Tel: 028 822 51500
info@nictt.org
www.nictt.co.uk
Northern Ireland charity for post traumatic stress and related illnesses and research. The Centre provides a trauma focused cognitive therapy treatment programme for people suffering from post traumatic stress disorder (PTSD) and related conditions. Subject to capacity this service is available to people affected by incidents linked to the Northern Ireland conflict (the Troubles) and other traumatic experiences.

Patient UK

www.patient.co.uk
Website with information about depression, schizophrenia, counselling, antidepressant drugs and self help, along with many links to articles and other resources.

PsychNet-UK

Tel: 0845 122 8622 (counselling line, 10.00am-1.00pm and 7.00pm-10.00pm, Monday to Friday)

www.psychnet-uk.com
A huge online source for medical information, including a section of mental health information and information on schizophrenia for professionals, families and students. Online support groups and links.

Refugee Support Centre

47 South Lambeth Road, London, SW8 1RH
Tel: 020 7820 3606
www.enabletogether.co.uk/charities/refugeesupportcentre.php
Part of the charity Enable Together. The Centre gives information and support for refugees, including counselling. Appointments are needed.

Relate UK

Tel: 0300 1001234
www.relate.org.uk
This charity offers advice, relationship counselling and sex therapy, and has workshops, mediation consulting and face-to-face or phone counselling. To find your nearest Relate office, telephone or use the online email form.

Relationships Scotland

18 York Place, Edinburgh, EH1 3EP

Tel: 0845 1192020
www.relationships-scotland.org.uk
The website states it's there for counselling, family mediation and family support. This Scottish charity was formed from the merger of Relate Scotland and Family Mediation Scotland. There is an email contact form on the website.

Saneline

1st Floor Cityside House, 40 Adler Street, London, E1 1EE
Tel: 0845 7678000 (saneline helpline)

020 7375 1002 (office)
info@sane.org.uk
www.sane.org.uk

Mental health charity which runs a national, out of hours telephone helpline providing information and support for anyone affected by mental health problems, including families and carers.

Schizophrenia.com

www.schizophrenia.com
An international website with a wealth of information on scizophrenia. Provides information, support and education for people with schizophrenia, families, caregivers and mental health professionals. Lots of information, with forums and discussion groups. You can also sign up for their newsletter.

The UK National Work Stress Network

9 Bell Lane, Syresham, Brackley, NN13 5HP
Tel: 07966196033
iandraper@nasuwt.net
www.workstress.net
Online tools, advice and guidance to help deal with stress in the workplace. Does not offer counselling but gives links to other organisations which do.

Workplace Bullying Support Group Network

Just Fight On, Crossbow Centre, 40 Liverpool Road, Slough, SL1 4QZ
Tel: 01753 593117
www.jfo.org.uk
Provides links to many support groups throughout the UK and Ireland for information and support about bullying in the workplace. Contact information, including website and email addresses, is available under each member group's link.

Professional organisations

British Association for Behavioural and Cognitive Psychotherapies (BABCP)

Victoria Buildings, 9-13 Silver Street, Bury, BL9 0EU
Tel: 0161 7974484

babcp@babcp.com
www.babcp.com
This site has a register of qualified practitioners and provides a series of informational pamphlets on a wide range of mental health issues from anxiety disorders, depression, phobias, schizophrenia, eating disorders, bipolar depression, as well as self help information. There is a small fee for the pamphlets.

British Association of Counselling and Psychotherapists

BACP House, 15 St John's Business Park, Lutterworth, Leicestershire, LE17 4HB
Tel: 01455 883316 (help desk)
01455 883300 (office)
bacp@bacp.co.uk
www.bacp.co.uk
Information for members of the public and health professionals. Sets standards for counselling and psychotherapy, and has a training section. Has articles about various mental health topics such as self-harm, depression and relationships. Has helpdesk service to help clients find therapists.

Irish Association for Counselling & Psychotherapy (IACP)

21 Dublin Road, Bray, County Wicklow, Republic of Ireland
Tel: 00 353 1 2723427
iacp@iacp.ie
www.irish-counselling.ie
Sets standards and criteria for counselling and psychotherapy in Ireland. Has a telephone referral helpline as well as information about counselling.

Mayo Clinic

www.mayoclinic.com
This is the site of the world famous Mayo Clinic in the USA, and contains a wealth of information about physical and mental health issues and treatments, as well as details on getting healthy and staying that way – there are even healthy eating recipes! The site offers a free e-newsletter. There is an email form on the contacts page.

Oxford Cognitive Therapy Centre (OCTC)

Oxford Cognitive Therapy Centre, Warneford Hospital, Oxford, OX3 7JX
Tel: 01865 223986
octc@obmh.nhs.uk
www.octc.co.uk
Based in the Oxford Psychology Department, part of Oxfordshire and Buckinghamshire Mental Health NHS Foundation Trust. This website gives information about a number of self help and information booklets on cognitive behavioural therapy for depression, obsessive compulsive disorder, bulimia nervosa and anorexia nervosa, anxiety disorders and others.

UK Council for Psychotherapy

2nd Floor, Edward House, 2 Wakley Street, London, EC1V 7LT
Tel: 020 7014 9955
info@ukcp.org.uk
www.psychotherapy.org.uk
This is an umbrella organisation with a register of psychotherapists and a 'find-a-therapist' service. The Council also works to encourage research, improve access to services, increase awareness of information and examine complaints against member organisations and therapists registered with the council.

World Health Organisation

Avenue Appia 20, 1211 Geneva 27, Switzerland
Tel: + 41 22 791 21 11
info@who.int
www.who.int/en
News about health, statistics, studies, research, outbreaks of disease, risk factors and health financing.

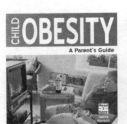

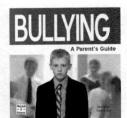
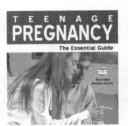
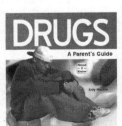